Hungarian Cookbook

Traditional Hungarian Recipes
Made Easy

www.grizzlypublishing.com

Table of Contents

Introduction

I want to thank you for purchasing this book, *'Hungarian Cookbook: Traditional Hungarian Recipes Made Easy.'*

Spicy, affluent and an extravaganza of different tastes, Hungary's food is a mouthwatering and amazing breakthrough for most travelers to the nationwide country. Developed over a large number of many years of Magyar background, traditional dishes continue being part of the abundant and proud ethnic heritage.

Hungarian cuisine is generally a mixture of fundamental peasant meals that originated many centuries back when nomadic tribes rode the amazing flatlands of Hungary, some new things that arrived with the Italians and Turks in the 15th and 16th centuries, and the elegant, highly developed cuisine which originated from the occasions of the Austro-Hungarian Empire. The result is a delicious, hearty, fare that aids Hungarians withstand extended, cold winters. Additionally, it is frequently incredibly indulgent, specifically when it entails pastries, desserts and cakes.

The Bulgarians and Turks were also accountable for introducing the most beloved and well-known spice of Hungary - paprika - in the 16th and 17th centuries. The Turks also launched filo pastry, tomatoes and sour cherries, which became important elements to the Hungarian kitchen.

Paprika, Hungary's piros 'crimson or arany platinum', can be an essential element of Hungarian food and it is the major taste. Not necessarily just is usually it used as a spices when planning foods but it additionally turns up on cafe furniture as a condiment next to the sodium and pepper shakers. You will find various types of dry out and refreshing paprika, but as a floor substance it is almost always many generally offered as csipőh or crisis roomőh ('warm' or 'solid') and édes (nice).

1

Probably the most well-known dish to result from Hungary is the paprika-laced meats stew known due to the fact gulyas (goulash); the name in fact means 'herdsmen' and arrived to become linked with the meats stew the herdsmen consumed. Kettle gulys (Bogracs gulyas) developed from learning to be a distributed hearty soup ready in a kettle on the fantastic Simple, to down the road getting an commendable market. Interestingly, 2 hundred years back when Hungary required a stand to safeguard its vocabulary, culture and gastronomy, gulyas became an indicator of the proud country and everyone consumed it - rich and poor. They still do today. And there are numerous variations on the theme - foods known as paprikas, tokany and porkolt.

Hungarians eat an astonishing level of meat (vegetarians, get sucked in: there's actually a dish called 'meat stuffed with meat'). Pig, meats, veal and poultry will be the meats most regularly consumed, and they can finish up being breaded and fried, prepared, simmered in locos (a delightful mixture of peppers, tomatoes and onions) or turned into some paprika-flavoured creation.

Typically the most popular dish prepared with paprika is gulyás or gulyásleves, a thick beef soup cooked with onions, cubed potatoes and paprika, and eaten as a primary program usually. Görkölt or 'stew' is certainly nearer to what all of those other globe calls 'goulash' & most typically produced with veal. Choose chicken, reduce the paprika just a little and add sour cream and - presto! - you have chicken paprikát. Eat these foods with galuska, basic dumplings produced with flour, or tarhonya, a barley-shaped egg pasta.

Chocolate became high for an artwork enter the changing times of the Austro-Hungarian Empire and exquisite confections were made - strudels filled up with apple, sour or sweet cherries, cream cheese, poppy seeds and walnuts; superior break up cakes like the beautiful dobostorta using its mahogany toffee leading; kugelhoph, beigli and many even more delights have been produced and acknowledged.

Chapter One: Hungarian Breakfast Recipes

Palatschinke (Hungarian Breakfast Crepes)

Serves: 2-4

Ingredients:

Crepes:

- 2 cups of whole wheat flour
- 2 medium eggs
- 1 cup milk
- 1 tablespoon coconut oil
- 1 tablespoon baking powder
- 1 cup sugar
- 2 tablespoon grated lemon zest
- 1 tablespoon vanilla extract

Filling:

- 1 cup of cottage cheese
- 2 tablespoon cinnamon
- Fruit of your choice

Method:

Crepes:

1. Put through a sieve and combine the dry ingredients in a large mixing bowl. Stir in eggs, milk, oil, lemon zest and vanilla until small bubbles start to form in batter and all the ingredients are mixed completely.

2. To prevent sticking, heat your medium-sized frying pan and add a teaspoon of coconut oil to it. Ladle in a three-quarter cup of the batter and tilt the pan to spread in a thin even coating.

3. When your batter turns to light brown and is covered in air holes, you know your crepe is ready to flip. Golden brown is your goal to know that both sides are done.

Filling:

1. Mix cottage cheese with cinnamon and fruit to your liking.

Rakott Kaposzta (Hungarian Cabbage Casserole)

Serves: 5

Ingredients:

- 1 large head of green cabbage
- 1 cup uncooked long grain rice
- 1 1/2 cups water
- 2 thick slices of uncooked bacon, diced
- 1 large onion, finely chopped
- 2 medium cloves garlic, minced
- 1 lb ground pork
- 1/4 cup water
- 1 tbsp Hungarian paprika
- 1/2 tbsp unsalted butter
- 16 ounces sour cream
- salt & pepper to taste

Method:

1. Remove the cabbage leaves carefully from the head and try to keep them as intact as possible. Remove any stem or core parts from the leaves (Your end goal is to have large pieces of cabbage leaves with no hard parts or stems).
2. Put 1 1/2 cups of water and rice into a small saucepan and cover it. Use medium-high heat to bring it to a boil, reduce the heat to low once it's boiling. Wait for about 5 minutes and then turn off the heat, let it rest for 10-15 minutes. It's important to not remove the lid during any of this process.
3. Prepare a large pot and place the cabbage leaves, add a sprinkle of salt and add some water until the cabbage is fully covered. Set the heat to medium and cook the

cabbage until it is tender. Turn off the heat and drain the cabbage, set it aside.

4. Prepare a large pan to cook the bacon, onion, and garlic for about 8-10 minutes over low-medium heat, until onion begins to brown and bacon, begins to crisp. Add the paprika, pork, 1/4 cup water, 1/2 tsp salt, 1/4 tsp pepper. Stir often with a wooden spoon to release any stuck-on bits, breaking up the ground pork and also scraping the bottom of the pan for about 5-7 minutes until pork is cooked. Add salt and pepper to taste or to your liking.

5. Preheat the oven to 400°F.

6. Prepare an 8x8 baking dish and rub the butter all over the bottom and sides.

7. Place 1/3 of the cabbage first, on the bottom of the dish. Put half the rice after and half the pork last. Place half the remaining cabbage on the pork and then spread half the sour cream on the cabbage. Then add the remaining rice then the remaining pork then the remaining cabbage and finally spread the remaining sour cream on top.

8. Use aluminum foil to cover the casserole and bake for about 20 minutes.

9. Remove the aluminum foil and bake for an additional 20-25 minutes or until edges start to brown.

10. Once you take it out from the oven, let it rest for about 10-15 minutes before serving.

Hungarian Omelet

Serves: 4

Ingredients:

- 1 yellow onion (medium, chopped)
- 1 cup sliced mushrooms
- 1/2 cup hungarian paprika (sweet)
- 5 tablespoons butter
- 6 eggs (beaten)
- 1/2 teaspoon salt
- 1/2 teaspoon ground pepper
- sour cream
- fresh parsley (chopped)
- green onion

Method:

1. Prepare a large frying pan over medium heat and put the butter until it melts, add the onion and sauté until it turns golden, then add the mushroom and paprika.
2. Cook the mushroom and paprika for about 5 minutes, stirring occasionally.
3. Prepare a small bowl to whisk the eggs, add a sprinkle of salt and pepper to taste.
4. Gently pour in the egg mixture in the pan over the top of the veggies. Cook it for about 10 minutes or until it is done enough to flip over without running.
5. Flip it again and cook the other side for about 3-4 minutes.
6. Cut the omelet to your liking and serve it with a dollop of sour cream and sprinkling of parsley and green onion.

Langos (Hungarian Fried Bread)

Serves: 4

Ingredients:

- 1 freshly boiled large potato, peeled, mash and kept warm
- 2 1/2 teaspoons instant yeast (same as rapid-rise or bread machine yeast)
- 1 3/4 cups all-purpose flour
- 1 tablespoon vegetable oil
- 1 teaspoon sugar
- 1/2 cup milk
- 2 cloves garlic (cut in half)
- 3/4 teaspoon salt

Method:

1. Put the freshly mashed warm potatoes, yeast, flour, oil, sugar, milk, and salt into a medium mixing bowl or stand mixer.
2. Mix the ingredients until they are well moistened.
3. Switch to the dough hook and knead for about 5 to 7 minutes or until smooth and elastic.
4. Move to a greased bowl, put a cover and let it rise until doubled.
5. Cut the dough into 4 portions equally and shape each piece into a smooth ball, lightly floured a board to place the dough. Put a cover and let it rest for about 20 minutes.
6. Prepare a large pan and heat the vegetable oil.
7. Take each dough ball, flatten and stretch to about an 8-inch diameter. Make 1 or more small slits in the center to help keep the dough from puffing up and not frying properly.

8. Fry langos one at a time for about 2 minutes for each side or until it turns golden. Drain the excess oil on paper towels.
9. Serve hot and rubbed with a cut of garlic clove and sprinkled with salt to taste.

Variations:

1. A savory variation would include a topping with sour cream and chopped dill or shredded cheese.
2. For those who like a sweeter variation, you can replace the garlic and salt with cinnamon or confectioners' sugar.

Savanyú Tojásleves (Hungarian Egg Drop Soup)

Serves: 2

Ingredients:

- 6 medium eggs
- 2 tablespoons oil
- 2 tablespoons flour
- 2 tablespoons sour cream
- 1 medium onion, finely chopped
- 1 tablespoon sweet paprika
- 1 bay leaf
- 1/2 tablespoon ground black pepper
- 1,2 l (~5 cups) water
- 1 – 1 1/2 tablespoons salt
- vinegar to taste

Method:

1. On a pot, heat up the oil then add the onions and flour, and make a blonde roux. Once it is done, put away the pot from the heat, put in paprika and stir slowly and then pour in water. While stirring regularly, add bay leaf, salt, and pepper. Cook for about 5-6 minutes, until onions are tender.
2. Whisk two eggs and gently pour them into the soup while stirring constantly. Let it continue to cook for about 1-2 minutes. Break one egg and pour it into the soup in one flowing movement. Repeat it with the rest of the eggs.
3. Leave them to cook for about 3-4 minutes, do not stir. Use a wooden spoon to gently move them to prevent sticking to the pot. Once the eggs are done, turn off the heat.

4. Mix the sour cream and some soup in a bowl until it is mixed properly, then pour slowly into the soup. Add a dash of vinegar to taste.

Rétese (Hungarian Strudel)

Serves: 4

Ingredients:

- 5 medium eggs
- 1 lb. our cherries or other fruits
- 2 1/4 cups cottage cheese
- 2 1/2 cups flour
- 2 cups milk
- 3/4 cup sour cream
- 1 1/2 cups powdered sugar
- 1/2 cup butter
- 2 tablespoons baking powder

Method:

1. Preheat your oven to 180°C.
2. Mix the flour, baking powder and powdered sugar in a medium bowl.
3. Rub the bottom of the baking pan with half of the butter and put half of the flour mixture into the baking pan. Cover the flour layer with cottage cheese, take a spoon of the sour cream and place it on top of the cottage cheese, then arrange the fruits on the sour cream layer.
4. Combine the rest of the flour mixture with the eggs and milk, and pour it over the layers in the baking pan. Crumb the butter over the top. Bake for about 50-60 minutes or until a cake tester comes out clean.
5. Let it cool and then cut into squares.

Note:
- Baking pan size: 30×40 cm / 12×15 inch.

Beigli (Hungarian Walnut Roll)

Serves: 12

Ingredients:

For the dough:

- 5 tablespoons white sugar
- 4 cups self-rising flour
- 3 egg yolks
- 1 (8 ounces) container sour cream
- 1 cup unsalted butter, cubed
- 1 (.25 ounce) package active dry yeast

For the filling:

- 2 1/2 cups finely chopped walnuts
- 1 egg
- 1 cup whole milk
- 1 cup white sugar
- 1 lemon, zested
- 2/3 cup golden raisins
- 1 tablespoon water

Method:

1. Combine the sugar, butter, egg yolks, and sour cream in the plate of a food processor installed with the dough knife and process well. Add the flour and yeast and process before dough all fits in place. If the dough feels too damp, add a bit more flour; whether it's too dried out, add dairy a tablespoon at the same time. The dough should be damp and easy to utilize.
2. Form the dough into a ball, cover with a wet towel, and reserve. To help make the filling up, heat the dairy and 1 glass glucose in a saucepan before sugars dissolves and

the combination has a syrupy regularity. Add the cut walnuts and mix to mix. Take away the saucepan from heat; mix in the lemon zest and raisins, and let filling up cool.

3. Separate the dough into three items. Roll one little bit of dough from a gently floured surface to create an extended rectangle in regards to a 1/4-in. thick; keep carefully the staying dough covered. Pass on 1/3 of the walnut filling up on the dough, departing about an inch of dough at each advantage. Move the dough up to create a log, and press to seal. Place the dough, seam-side down, on the parchment-lined cooking sheet. Do it again with the rest of the dough and filling up.

4. Defeat the egg with the tablespoon of drinking water to make an egg clean. Clean the loaves with egg clean and let rest for one hour in a warm place. When the dough has increased, clean it again with egg clean and put the cooking holder in the refrigerator for thirty minutes (this gives the dough a gleaming finish).

5. Preheat an oven to 375 F (190 C).

6. Bake the loaves until they're a deep golden dark brown, about 35 to 45 minutes.

Kalács (Hungarian Braided Sweet Bread)

Serves: 6

Ingredients:

- 4 cups flour
- 3 1/2 tablespoons melted butter
- 2 1/2 teaspoons dry yeast
- 2 teaspoons salt
- 1 cup lukewarm milk
- 1 egg + 1 egg yolk
- 1 egg for egg wash
- 1/3 cup sugar

Method:

1. Place yeast and 1 teaspoon of sugar in a small bowl and dissolve in 100 ml of lukewarm milk.
2. Sift flour in a separate bowl, make a hollow in it and add the ingredients: milk, sugar, salt, egg, egg yolk, and the activated yeast. Use your hand or a mixer and start to knead. When the ingredients are well combined and the dough starts to form a ball, add melted butter to the dough in small amounts and continue to knead until all the butter is incorporated and the dough is smooth, pliant and not sticky. Cover and leave to rise until it doubles in size (it takes about 40-50 minutes).
3. Turn out the dough on a floured surface, divide it into 6 (or less) equal pieces and form balls. Cover them and let them rise for 10 minutes, so the gluten threads can stretch out and dough can be rolled out easier. Roll them into 40 cm long ropes. Pinch the tops of the 6 ropes together and braid them into a bread shape. You can google the braiding technique and I found this video that shows how to braid a 6-strand sweet bread.

4. Line a baking sheet with parchment and lift the bread on it. Brush it with beaten egg and let it rise for 30-40 minutes. Preheat the oven to 180 °C. Brush the bread with egg again, and slide it on its baking sheet into the oven. Bake for 40 minutes.
5. Let it cool on a wire rack until just barely warm.

Töltött Tojás (Deviled Eggs)

Serves: 6

Ingredients:

- 6 large hard-boiled eggs, cooled and peeled (make use of higher omega-eggs if available; you'll only use half the yolks)
- 2 tablespoons red pepper (finely chopped)
- 2 teaspoons green onion (finely chopped, mostly the green part)
- 2 tablespoons light mayonnaise (or any mayonnaise to your liking)
- 2 teaspoons Dijon mustard
- 1/4 cup crab, cleaned and shredded (or finely chopped lean ham)
- 1/2 teaspoon parsley flakes
- a small amount ground nutmeg
- black pepper to taste

Method:

1. Cut eggs in two lengthwise and take away the yolks. Place half the yolks in a medium dish and mash with fork.
2. Add the crab, red pepper, green onion, mayonnaise, mustard, nutmeg, and parsley to the yolks and mix well with a fork. Add pepper to flavor.
3. Spoon mixture evenly among the 12 egg white halves

Halászlé (Fisherman's Soup)

Serves: 3

Ingredients:

- 2 lb. fresh-water fish, sliced
- 2 tablespoons sweet ground paprika
- 2 medium onions, finely chopped
- 1 green pepper
- 1 medium tomato
- 1 – 1 1/2 tablespoons salt
- 6-7 pt. water
- 3/4 cup tarhonya (egg barley)
- 1/4 tablespoons hot ground paprika

Method:

1. Place the seafood pieces and water in a bogrács or container.
2. Add finely cut onion and take it to a boil. When the water comes, add paprika (excess fat of the seafood releases by that point and paprika can dissolve in it), salt, the entire green pepper and entire tomato. Over low warmth simmer gradually for 2 hours; shake the bogrács or container every once in a while, do not mix the soup to avoid damaging the seafood slices.
3. Add egg barley 20 minutes prior to the two-hour cooking food time concludes, and keep simmering before noodles are sensitive.
4. Serve hot, with white breads and hot green pepper pieces.

Karalábéleves (Hungarian Creamy Kohlrabi Soup)

Serves: 2

Ingredients:

- 1 big kohlrabi (1 lb.)
- 2 level teaspoon salt or 3 level teaspoon homemade vegetable seasoning *(See note)*
- 2 parsley roots
- 1 carrot
- 1 tablespoon oil
- 1 egg
- 6 cups water
- pinch of lovage
- small bunch of parsley
- 1/4 cup soft butter
- 3/4 cup flour

Method:

1. Peel and cube the kohlrabi, carrot and parsley roots.
2. Slowly heat the oil in a medium sized pot.
3. Add the kohlrabi, carrot and parsley root cubes.
4. Sprinkle with salt or seasoning.
5. Add a couple of tablespoons of water to sauté the vegetables. Keep an eye on the heat to make sure the vegetables don't get brown. Add more liquid if the water boils away. Stir often.
6. When the vegetables are tender, add water and lovage.
7. Bring the soup to a slow simmer.
8. Meanwhile prepare the batter of the dumplings.
9. Combine the egg, soft butter and flour.
10. Beat to form a smooth and pliable batter.

11. Push the batter through a dumpling maker into the soup. Or you can simply use a spoon to make small dumplings and drop them into the soup.
12. Cook for 2-3 minutes.
13. Turn off the heat, add the chopped parsley to the soup and it's ready to serve.

Note:

Homemade vegetable seasoning:

Ingredients:

- 500 g (~1 lb) carrot
- 500 g (~1 lb) parsley root
- 500 g (~1 lb) red pepper
- 200 g (~7 oz) celeriac
- 100 g (~3 1/2 oz) cauliflower
- 100 g (~3 1/2 oz) red onion
- 100 g (~3 1/2 oz) tomato
- 100 g (~3 1/2 oz) kohlrabi
- 1 head of garlic
- 1 large bunch of parsley
- 1 large bunch of celeriac leaves
- Salt

Method:

1. Wash and clean the vegetables, then cut them into large pieces.
2. Push them through a meat grinder.
3. Measure the weight of the mixture.
4. Add 150 g (~2/3 cup) salt for every kilo of minced vegetables and mix up.
5. Wait until the mixture gives off juice, it takes about 30 minutes.

6. Spoon the blend into jars (preferably choose small ones). Press the mixture with spoon repeatedly to make it airtight.
7. Close the jars and put them onto the pantry shelf. Store in a cool, dark place in order to prevent the seasoning from losing its color.

Hungarian Lentil Soup

Serves: 8

Ingredients:

- 7 cups chicken stock
- 3 carrots, diced
- 3 1/2 cups crushed tomatoes
- 2 bay leaves
- 2 tablespoons olive oil
- 2 large onions, cubed
- 2 stalks celery, diced
- 1 1/2 cups lentils - soaked, rinsed and drained
- 1 sprig fresh parsley, chopped
- 1 teaspoon minced garlic
- 1/2 teaspoon salt
- 1/2 teaspoon ground black pepper
- 1/2 teaspoon paprika
- 1/2 cup grated Parmesan cheese
- 3/4 cup white wine

Method:

1. In a large stockpot, sauté the onions in oil until they are glossy. Stir in garlic, paprika, celery, carrots, and sauté for 10 minutes.
2. Once the vegetables have sautéed for 10 minutes stir in tomatoes, chicken stock, lentils, bay leaves, salt, and pepper. Stir well, then add the wine and bring the mixture to a boil. Slowly reduce the heat and cook for 1 hour on low to medium heat; or until the lentils are tender.
3. Sprinkle the soup with parsley and Parmesan (optional) before serving.

Tarhonyaleves (Hungarian Egg Barley Soup)

Serves: 2

Ingredients:

- 8 cups water
- 7 oz potatoes, diced
- 3 1/2 oz dry egg barley
- 1 oz smoked bacon, chopped
- 1 tablespoon paprika
- 1 tomato, peeled and chopped
- 1 wax pepper, sliced
- 1 tablespoon salt
- a small bunch of parsley, finely chopped

Method:

1. Within a container, fry cut bacon until crispy. Add egg fry and barley in the bacon extra fat - stirring constantly - until its color becomes light dark brown.
2. Remove from heat, sprinkle with paprika and present it a good mix to layer the egg barley. Pour in 2 liters / 8 mugs of drinking water and go back to heat (if the noodles absorb too much drinking water during cooking food, feel absolve to add more drinking water).
3. Add salt, wax and tomato pepper. When the egg barley is prepared, add diced potatoes and make before potatoes and noodles are sensitive.
4. Switch off heat and sprinkle the soup with finely cut parsley.

Hunza Bread

Serves: 20

Ingredients:

- 8 cups bread flour
- 6 egg yolks
- 3 (.25 ounce) packages active dry yeast
- 2 teaspoons salt
- 2 egg whites, beaten
- 1 1/2 cups white sugar
- 1 1/2 cups warm milk
- 1 cup warm water (110 degrees F/45 degrees C)
- 1 cup margarine, melted
- 1 cup golden raisins

Method:

1. In a small bowl, dissolve yeast in warm water. Let stand until creamy, about 10 minutes.
2. In a large bowl, mix together flour, sugar and salt. Make a well in the center of the flour and pour in the yeast mixture, egg yolks, margarine and warm milk. Stir until a soft dough is formed. Turn it out onto a lightly floured surface and knead until smooth and supple, about 6 minutes. Lightly oil a large bowl, place the dough in the bowl and turn to coat with oil. Cover with a damp cloth and let rise in a warm place until doubled in volume, about 1 hour.
3. Deflate the dough and turn it out onto a lightly floured surface. Knead in the raisins. Divide the dough into two equal pieces and form into loaves. Place the loaves into two lightly greased 9x5 inch loaf pans. Cover the loaves with a damp cloth and let rise until doubled in volume, about 40 minutes. Meanwhile, preheat oven to 350 degrees F (175 degrees C).

4. Brush the risen loaves with egg whites. Bake in preheated oven for 30 to 45 minutes, until golden brown.

Lecsó (Hungarian Tomato-Pepper Stew)

Serves: 5

Ingredients:

- 2 tablespoons bacon grease (or oil)
- 1 onion (medium, sliced thinly)
- 1-pound banana (Hungarian wax, Italian or green bell peppers, cut into 1/4-inch strips)
- 3 large tomatoes (peeled and chopped)
- 1 1/2 teaspoons sugar
- 1 1/2 teaspoons salt (less if using sausage)
- 1 tablespoon sweet hungarian paprika

Method:

1. In a large skillet, sauté the onion in bacon fat or oil over low heat for 5 minutes.
2. Add pepper strips and cook another 15 minutes.
3. Add tomatoes, sugar, salt and paprika and cook for another 25 to 30 minutes, stirring occasionally, or until mixture resembles chunky tomato sauce.

Hungarian Farsangi Fánk

Serves: 24

Ingredients:

- 5 egg yolks (slightly whisk)
- 5 1/4 cups flour (sifted)
- 2 1/4 teaspoon active dry yeast
- 2 cups milk (warmed)
- 1 teaspoon salt
- 1 tablespoon granulated sugar
- 1/2 cup unsalted butter (melted)
- canola oil for frying
- confectioners' sugar for sprinkling

Method:

1. Add 1/4 glass of the warm dairy to the plate of a stand mixer installed with the dough hook connection. Sprinkle the dairy with the yeast and the sugars. Mix softly with a spoon and let are a symbol of 15 minutes. Mixture should show up foamy after a few moments.
2. Add the melted butter to the rest of the dairy. Combine the dairy combination with the egg yolks, sodium and the yeast blend. Mix in two the flour and blend well. Mix in the rest of the flour and knead before dough is easy and elastic and begins to distance themselves from the dish. The dough should be a little sticky.
3. Form the dough into a ball and place in a big dish sprayed with non-stick cooking aerosol. Cover the dish with plastic cover and let rise in a warm place until doubled in mass, about 45 minutes. (I preheat my oven to 200 levels and then transform it off.)
4. After dough is doubled in proportions, punch down and place dough on gently floured surface. Move dough out

to 1/2 in. thick. Utilizing a 3-inch circle, slice out doughnuts. Re-roll scraps.

5. Line 2 large cooking linens with parchment paper. Place 12 doughnuts on each sheet. Cover doughnuts with kitchen towels and let rest for approximately 30 minutes.

6. Pour enough canola essential oil, about 1-2 quarts, into a huge heavy bottomed Dutch oven so it is a few ins deep, arranged over medium-low warmth. When essential oil is hot enough, add 4 doughnuts at the same time and make for approximately 2 minutes per part until fantastic. Remove doughnuts from oil with a slotted spoon and place on a rack over a sizable baking sheet. Repeat with staying doughnuts.

7. Sprinkle warm doughnuts with confectioners' sugar.

8. Serve warm.

Hungarian Style Scrambled Eggs

Serves: 2

Ingredients:

- 4 eggs
- 2 onion
- 2 strips of real bacon
- 1 teaspoon marjoram
- 1 teaspoon red paprika
- salt and pepper to taste

Method:

1. Roughly chop the bacon and begin to fry it on a medium high temperature and render some fat.
2. Add the onions, add salt and cook them until they may be caramelized
3. Add the red paprika, mix and add the eggs.
4. Once you add the eggs, take away the skillet from heat and allow the eggs cook from heat source. Usually this will give you a creamy but well-cooked egg.

Gofri (Hungarian Waffles)

Serves: 4

Ingredients:

- 12 oz milk
- 4 medium eggs
- 2 teaspoons baking powder
- 1 teaspoon vanilla sugar
- 1/2 lb. flour
- 1/5 lb. sugar
- 1/3 lb. butter

Method:

1. Melt the butter.
2. Put all the ingredients and mix them well.
3. Prepare the waffle maker and heat it, and pour into it from the mixture, with a smaller ladle.
4. Serve when ready with maple syrup, honey, chocolate syrup or jam.

Bálmos

Serves: 8

Ingredients:

- 400 ml (1 2/3 cups) cream
- 120 g (2 1/2 oz) polenta (coarsely ground cornmeal)
- 100 g (3 1/2 oz) sheep milk cheese
- 100 ml (1/2 cup) sour cream
- 80 g (3 oz) bacon
- 20 g (1 1/5 tbsp) butter
- 1/2 teaspoon salt to taste

Method:

1. Chop and fry bacon until crispy. Put it aside.
2. Place cream, sour cream and salt in a saucepan and take it to a moving boil. When bubbles aplenty burst, mix in cornmeal. Decrease the heat to low setting and cook while stirring regularly. Once cornmeal is nearly tender and solid enough, start stirring until grease sweats out vigorously. Add butter to the hot dish and keep combining until butter melts.
3. Once it's smooth and tender, switch off heat and put from the grease in a little bowl. With 2 spoons form dumplings from the polenta and put them onto a platter. Sprinkle the drained grease on the dumplings, then scatter crumbled sheep dairy cheese and crispy bacon around them.
4. Serve right away.

Chapter Two: Hungarian Lunch Recipes

Zoli Bacsi Salataja (Zoli's Iceberg and Speck Salad)

Serves: 4

Ingredients:

- 1 iceberg lettuce (core removed)
- 100 g smoked speck *(see note,* cut into lardons)
- 1 teaspoon caster sugar
- 1 tablespoon white wine vinegar

Method:

1. Remove leaves from lettuce and place in a colander. Pour over boiling drinking water until leaves begin to wilt. Refresh under chilly running water, then drain and transfer to a big bowl.
2. Place sugar, vinegar and 2 tablespoons of water in a little bowl and stir until sugar dissolves. Pour over lettuce and toss with speck.
3. Refrigerate until prepared to serve.

Note:

- Eastern European-style smoked speck is greatly smoked than other types and therefore will not require cooking. It really is available from delis and chosen supermarkets. Alternative bacon or other speck, cut into lardons and pan-fry until it turns brown.

Hungarian Hen Soup in Újházy Style

Serves: 6

Ingredients:

- 1 chicken (2-3 lb.)
- 2,5-3 l water
- 1 1/2 oz celeriac
- 1 3/4 oz kohlrabi
- 1 3/4 oz savoy cabbage
- 1 3/4 oz mushrooms
- 3 1/2 oz cauliflowers
- 5 oz green peas
- 3 1/2 oz vermicelli
- 3 parsley roots
- 2 pinches of saffron or safflower
- 2 medium carrots
- 2-3 tablespoons salt
- 2 garlic cloves
- 1 teaspoon lovage
- 1 small onion
- 1 sweet green pepper
- 1 medium tomato
- 10-14 peppercorns

Method:

1. Clean the hen and wash it, then it cut into parts.
2. Clean, peel off and rinse the vegetables. Slice the carrots, parsley origins, kohlrabi and celeriac in bigger parts.
3. Put the meat in a big pot and cover with approximately 2,5-3 l of cool water. Place over heat without a cover and take it to the boil.
4. Skim the foam from the very best of water.

5. Put pepper corns, garlic saffron and cloves or safflower in a tea ball.
6. Add 2 tsps. of sodium, the tea ball, onion and lovage to the soup. Cover with a cover and begin to simmer on low warmth. After 40-45 minutes add carrots, parsley root base, celeriac, kohlrabi, savoy cabbage (not cut), entire green pepper and tomato (and sodium if needed). Simmer before meats gets completely smooth.
7. Drain the soup utilizing a colander. Take away the bigger bones from the meats and keep it warm by covering with 2-3 ladles of soup.
8. Dispose of savoy cabbage, onion, green pepper, tomato and this content of the tea ball. Place the boiled vegetables onto a dish and reserve.
9. Make the cauliflowers, peas and mushrooms in 1-2 ladles of soup in a smaller container. If it's ready, add the boiled vegetables.
10. Pour 1 litre of soup in another container and prepare the vermicelli.
11. Add the meats, boiled vermicelli and vegetables in a soup tureen and cover with soup.
12. Serve immediately.

Pörkölt (Hungarian Stew) Made with Pork

Serves: 14

Ingredients:

- 5 bacon pieces (diced)
- 5 lb. boneless pork chops (trimmed)
- 2 medium-large onions (diced)
- 14 oz diced tomatoes, with liquid
- 2 mugs reduced-fat sour cream
- 6 oz large egg noodles
- 1 large yellow bell pepper (seeded and diced)
- 1/2 teaspoons garlic powder
- 1/4 cup Hungarian paprika
- 1/4 teaspoon pepper to taste
- 2/3 cup beef broth

Method:

1. Place the bacon in a big, deep skillet, and cook it over medium-high temperature until browned equally, about ten minutes. Drain, and reserve the drippings. Add the onions to the bacon and prepare before onion is translucent. Remove skillet from the stove and mix the paprika, garlic powder, and pepper in to the bacon mix. Transfer the mix into a huge stockpot.

2. Heat a little amount of the reserved bacon drippings in the skillet again over medium-high temperature. Make the pork chops in batches in the hot drippings until evenly browned on both relative edges. Use additional bacon drippings for every batch as needed. Take away the pork chops to a slicing panel and blot surplus fat off the top of chops with a paper towel; lower into bite-sized cubes and mix in to the bacon mixture.

3. Heat a little amount of the bacon drippings in the skillet; make and mix the bell pepper in the hot drippings until fragrant and softened; drain on the dish lined with paper towels. Mix the prepared pepper in to the bacon mixture.

4. Pour the tomatoes with liquid and beef broth into a location and stockpot the container over medium-high heat. Bring to a simmer and reduce high temperature to medium-low. Make before stew starts to thicken, stirring sometimes, about 90 minutes. Stir the sour cream in to the stew before offering just.

5. Bring a pot with lightly-salted drinking water and bring to a moving boil; add the egg noodles to the come back and drinking water to a boil. Make uncovered, stirring sometimes, before pasta through has prepared, but is company to the bite still, about five minutes. Drain well in a colander occur the kitchen sink. Ladle the stew within the drained noodles to provide.

Hungarian Chicken Paprikash

Serves: 4

Ingredients:

- chicken piece (breasts, legs, or thighs, with bones)
- 3 tablespoons Hungarian paprika (preferably Szeged)
- 3 tablespoons vegetable oil
- 2 cups chicken broth
- 1 cup sour cream
- 1 cup chopped onion
- 1/2 cup flour
- 1/8 teaspoon ground red pepper (cayenne)
- salt and pepper to taste

Method:

1. Combine flour, 2 tablespoons paprika, pepper and salt.
2. Dredge chicken parts in flour combination.
3. Reserve the rest of the flour.
4. Add oil to large dutch oven.
5. Heat it oil over medium-high temperature.
6. Add the chicken and cook until dark brown on both sides, approx. 10 minutes.
7. Remove the chicken from pot.
8. Add little oil to container (if bottom is apparently too dried out).
9. Add onion, red pepper, 1 tablespoon paprika, and sodium.
10. Saute until onion is delicate, approx. 2 minutes.
11. Bring back the chicken to the container, and add enough chicken broth to immerse.
12. Bring to boil, reduce the temperature, cover, and simmer about 30 to 45 minutes, until chicken is done.
13. Remove from heat and let paprikash cool off.

14. Combine the left-over flour and 1/2 glass sour cream.
15. Add little bit of liquid from pot into flour mix and mixt with whisk until smooth.
16. Add the mix to the container, stirring constantly.
17. Simmer for five minutes.
18. Let it cool off and add the rest of the sour cream again, stirring constantly.
19. The color of the sauce should be a very pale orange color (almost white).
20. Cook for about 1 minute until warmed.
21. Serve over homemade Hungarian nokedli (spaetzel), wide egg noodles, or cooked cavatelli.

Authentic Hungarian Goulash

Serves: 6

Ingredients:

- 4 medium-large potatoes (peeled and cubed)
- 2 pounds flank steak
- 2 tablespoons butter
- 2 large onions (diced)
- 1 clove garlic, minced
- 1/8 teaspoon caraway seed
- 1/4 teaspoon dried marjoram
- 5 tablespoons paprika
- 2 cups water
- salt and pepper to taste

Method:

1. Melt butter in a big soup container over medium-high temperature. Saute onions until smooth, then add meat and brown. Mix in caraway seed, marjoram, paprika and garlic. Pour water over everything, lower heat to low and simmer for 2 1/2 hours.
2. Add potatoes and cook until soft, at least one 45 minutes to 1 hour. Season with salt and pepper to flavor and
3. Serve while hot.

amazon.co.uk®

A gift from **Kate xxx**

Dearest Christine, Thank you for a really special trip and for all of your support. Lots of love xx From Kate xxx

Gift note included with **Hungarian Cookbook: Traditional Hungarian Recipes Made Easy**

Langalló – The Hungarian Pizza

Serves: 4

Ingredients:

- 500 g (4 cups) flour
- 300 ml (1 1/4 cups) sour cream
- 300 ml (1 1/4 cups) water
- 200 g (7 oz) goat cheese or sheep's milk cheese
- 200 g (7 oz) smoked sausage
- 200 g (7 oz) smoked bacon
- 20 g (2 teaspoons) fresh or dry yeast
- 3 tablespoons melted lard
- 2 red onions
- pinch of sugar
- 1 teaspoon salt

Method:

1. Put yeast, sugar, one tablespoon of flour and 100 ml of lukewarm drinking water in a little bowl and allow it rest until it dissolves.
2. Sift the rest of the flour in another bowl, add salt, activated yeast and the remaining lukewarm water, and with a hand's mixer, knead the dough until it begins to hold together. Keep on kneading while steadily pouring in the melted lard. The dough is ready whenever a ball form. Cover with a kitchen towel and allow it to triple in size.
3. Separate the dough into six equivalent parts, form balls, cover and let them rise for ten minutes. Roll them out into circles with a diameter of 20-25 cm. You are able to choose if you pre-bake the bases in the oven pre-heated to 200 °C or place them one at a time in a dried-out frying

pan that is on a higher heat and toast their both of their sides about for 2 minutes on the stove.

4. When the circles are pre-baked, pass on a thin coating of sour cream on top, add sausage pieces, bacon, thinly sliced up red onion and cheese. Place the "pizzas" on cooking linens lined with parchment paper, slip them in to the oven and bake them for ten minutes.

5. When the cheese melts and the crust change color, Langalló is ready to serve.

Hungarian Cottage Cheese Noodles

Serves: 4

Ingredients:

- 5 bacon slices
- 3 cups uncooked noodle (any noodle to your liking)
- 1 cup sour cream
- 1 cup cottage cheese
- 1/2 cup cheese (optional)
- 1 teaspoon salt and pepper to taste

Method:

1. Boil water for the noodle and add some salt
2. Mix the sour cream with the cottage cheese.
3. Chop the bacon stripes to small size pieces.
4. Cook them on a pan and stir them constantly to avoid burning.
5. Cook the noodle.
6. Put the fried bacon bits on a paper towel to absorb any excess fat.
7. Drain your noodles.
8. Serve the noodles with the sour cream and cottage cheese mixture, then sprinkle it with the grated cheese and bacon bits.

Bugaci Borsós Betyár

Serves: 4

Ingredients:

- 500 g (1 lb.) pork
- 250 g (1/2 lb.) frozen green peas
- 200 g (7 oz) bacon
- 3 tablespoons sour cream
- 3/4 tablespoon lard
- 1 medium onion
- 1 tablespoon mustard
- 1 tablespoon paprika cream
- freshly ground black pepper to taste
- a small bunch of parsley

Method:

1. Dice bacon and pork, chop the onion. Heat lard in a pan, add bacon and fry until crispy. Stir in finely chopped onion and sauté until translucent. Put the pork and cook until all sides turn to white. Add a dash of black pepper, pour in a little bit of water, cover and cook slowly. Add more water as required.
2. Once the meat is almost tender, add green peas, mustard, sour cream and paprika cream, and cook until it's done. Turn off the heat and sprinkle with finely chopped parsley.
3. Serve with steamed rice.

Note:

- Since bacon and paprika cream are salty, carefully handle the salt. First taste, then add salt if necessary.

Stefánia Vagdalt (Meatloaf Stuffed with Egg)

Serves: 5

Ingredients:

- 5 hardboiled eggs
- 600 g (1 1/3 lb.) ground pork
- 2 eggs
- 1-2 slices of white bread
- 100 ml milk
- 3 garlic cloves, grated
- 2 tablespoons oil
- 2 tablespoons paprika
- 2 teaspoon finely chopped parsley leaves
- 1 large onion (finely sliced)
- 1 teaspoon pepper
- 1 tablespoon salt
- 1 egg for the egg wash

Method:

1. Soak the bread slices in dairy. Make hardboiled eggs. Preheat the oven to 200°C.
2. Pour the oil in a skillet and sauté the onions until translucent. Press the milk-soaked loaf of bread. Place the pork in a dish, add sautéed onions, grated garlic, two eggs, squeezed breads, paprika, pepper, salt and finely cut parsley, and combine thoroughly.
3. Peel off the hardboiled eggs. Line a cooking sheet with parchment paper.
4. Place 1 / 3 of the meat's combination on the cooking sheet and form a 10 cm/4 in wide rectangle. Place the hardboiled eggs in a row in the center. Cover the eggs with the remaining meat and form it into a loaf, then brush with beaten egg.

5. Bake the meatloaf for one hour.
6. Serve it hot or cold.

Szárma (Hungarian Stuffed Cabbage)

Serves: 4

Ingredients:

- 500 g (1 lb.) minced pork
- 200 g (7 oz) rice
- 100 g (3 1/2 oz) smoked bacon (finely chopped)
- 2,5 – 3 l (10-12 cups) tomato juice or 500 ml (2 cups) tomato purée
- 2 medium-large heads of cabbage
- 2 tablespoons oil or lard
- 2 garlic cloves (crushed)
- 1 big onion (finely chopped)
- 1/2 tablespoon paprika
- 1/2 teaspoon black pepper
- 1 – 1 1/2 teaspoon salt
- 2 pinches of ground caraway

Method:

1. Bring a big pot of water to a boil. Take away the external leaves of the cabbage and core out of the heads. Place a head (cored part up) in the boiling water and wait until you can simply peel off the leaves with a solid wood spoon one at a time. Get them out from the water. Take off the hard rib from the bottom of every cabbage leaf, then lengthwise slice the leaves in two (your goal is to make only a small amount roll as you possibly can). Repeat the above-mentioned process with the other cabbages.

2. As the leaves cool, prepare the stuffing. Sauté the finely cut onion in oil or lard. Once it's done, switch off heat and sprinkle the onion with paprika. Set aside and let it cool a bit. Place minced pork and finely cut bacon in a dish.

Wash the rice and add it to the meats. Add garlic and sautéed onion. Season with salt, ground and pepper caraway. Blend them up with your hands.

3. Place a little amount of stuffing on each leaf, move it up and softly tuck in the ends. When all the stuffing is fully gone, cut the staying cabbage leaves into fine shreds.

4. Put half of the cut cabbage into a huge container. Arrange the cabbage rolls at the top, seam side down, and scatter the rest of the cabbage over them. Pour in tomato juice sufficient to cover the meals; if you are using tomato purée, dilute it with water and put in the cabbage. Take it to a boil, decrease the heat, cover the container and gradually simmer for approximately 2 hours.

5. Serve the cabbage rolls with sour cream and breads.

Hungarian Casino Egg Salad

Serves: 5

Ingredients:

- 6 hardboiled eggs (cut in half)
- 3 tablespoons butter (unsalted, melted and slightly cooled)
- 3 tablespoons sour cream
- 3 anchovy fillets loaded in oil (minced and drained)
- 2 teaspoons distilled white vinegar
- 1 tablespoon capers (chopped)
- 1 tablespoon fresh chives (snipped)
- 1 tablespoon red onion (finely chopped, or shallot)
- 1/4 teaspoon freshly ground black pepper

Method:

1. Scoop the yolks from the halved eggs and put them in a medium bowl. Add the butter, sour cream, vinegar, and pepper. Whisk together until a creamy, smooth paste forms.
2. Coarsely chop the egg whites and add them to the egg yolk mixture, along with the anchovies, capers, chives and red onion. Gently fold the ingredients until fully mixed.
3. Serve right away, or put a cover and refrigerate until it's ready to serve.
4. The egg salad can be made up to 3 days in advance.

Hungarian Grilled Cheese Sandwich

Serves: 4

Ingredients:

- 1 baguette
- 8 sour dill pickles (thinly sliced)
- 8 slices salami (Hungarian, mild or spicy)
- 4 oz. swiss cheese (sliced)
- 1/2 teaspoon hungarian paprika

Method:

1. Cut baguette in half, lengthwise and partway through.
2. Fill baguette with cheese, pickles and salami. Sprinkle with paprika and close.
3. Cut baguette sandwich into 4 pieces.
4. Heat the frying pan over medium-low heat and cook all 4 pieces, about 8 minutes on each side. Put a little pressure on them, until cheese is melted and baguette is crispy and browned.

Hungarian Style Burger

Serves: 4

Ingredients:

- 1 lb. beef sirloin (fine quality ground, and chuck mix)
- 4 kaiser rolls (toasted)
- 1 tablespoon dry red wine
- 1 tablespoon flat leaf parsley (chopped)
- 1 tablespoon paprika (sweet red, Hungarian)
- 1 pinch kosher salt (and fresh ground black pepper)
- 1/2 teaspoon lemon zest (fresh)
- 1/4 cup red onion (chopped)
- 1/2 teaspoon fresh thyme leaves
- 1/2 cup sour cream (for garnish)
- sprinkle of sweet paprika (garnish)
- 1 sprig fresh thyme and parsley (garnish)

Method:

1. Prepare your grill.
2. Mix your beef, herbs, spices, salt, wine, and lemon zest together and shape into 4 patties.
3. Grill 2-4 minutes per side, depending upon your thickness, heat of the grill, and desired level of "doneness."
4. Garnish with sour cream, herbs, and a sprinkle of sweet paprika.
5. Serve them on a toasted roll, such as a Kaiser roll or to your liking.

Krumplis Tészta (Hungarian Potato Pasta)

Serves: 4

Ingredients:

- 4 medium-large potatoes
- 300 grams pasta (to your liking)
- 2 cloves garlic
- 2 tablespoons paprika powder
- 2 tablespoons olive oil (optional)
- 1 onion
- salt and pepper to taste
- pickles (to serve)

Method:

1. Chop onion and garlic very finely and sauté them on oil or in water until tender.
2. Cut potatoes into very small cubes and add to the sautéed onion with paprika powder.
3. Stir for a few seconds, then pour in water to cover potatoes. Cook for about 15-20 minutes.
4. Meanwhile prepare your pasta according to package instructions.
5. Once potatoes are totally soft and the water is almost completely evaporated, mash potatoes roughly with a fork. Season with salt and a lot of pepper.
6. Stir pasta into the potato mixture and serve warm with pickles.

Gyuvecs

Serves: 4

Ingredients:

- 8 thin slices of boneless pork
- 4 medium potatoes
- 500 g (1 lb.) tomatoes
- 500 g (1 lb.) wax peppers
- 200 g (1 cup) rice
- 450 g (1 3/4 cups) sour cream
- 3 tablespoons lard
- 1 medium-big onion
- salt and pepper to taste

Method:

1. Boil the potatoes on a medium heat until tender, leave their skin on. Drain, set it aside and let it cool.
2. Cook the rice in salty water, then set aside.
3. Dice the onion, chop tomatoes and wax peppers coarsely. Peel the tomatoes and slice a shallow "X" cut in the bottom of each tomato, then put them into a pot of boiling water. Boil until the skin starts to wrinkle and split, then take them out with a slotted spoon and move them to a cold-water bath. After that, use your fingers to peel the tomato skins.
4. Cut 2-3 slits on the edges of each pork slice to prevent them from curling, then salt and pepper them. Prepare a frying pan and heat the lard, cook the pork until both sides turn golden brown. Transfer meat onto a plate, and make lecsó.
5. Add finely chopped onion to the hot lard left in the frying pan. Sauté until translucent, then add coarsely chopped wax peppers. Cook it for approx. 8-10 minutes, then stir

in the tomatoes. Season with a sprinkle of salt and pepper, and cook until soft.

6. Peel and slice the boiled potatoes. Grease an oven-proof dish thoroughly. Put half of the potatoes into the half bottom part of the dish, spoon rice and put it into the other half of the bottom and smooth it out. Sprinkle with salt. Lay the pork over them, then cover the meat with lecsó. Complete layering by putting the remaining potatoes and rice on top of the lecsó. Salt and spread the top with sour cream. Put them in the oven and cook for about 20-25 minutes at 200°C until sour cream turns light pink.

Májas Hurka (Hungarian Sausage)

Serves: 4

Ingredients:

- 2 kg (4 1/2 lbs.) pork liver
- 1 pork lung (1 lb.)
- 800 g (1 3/4 lbs.) rice
- 700-800 g (1 1/2 – 1 3/4 lbs.) unsmoked bacon (e.g. jowl)
- 300-400 g (2/3 – 3/4 lb.) fatty meat (e.g. shoulder)
- 2-3 big onions
- 2 tablespoons lard
- 1 tablespoon paprika
- approx. 5-6 m natural casings (small intestines)
- approx. 80-90 g (2 3/4 oz) salt (or to taste)
- approx. 40-60 g (1 1/2 – 2 oz) ground black pepper (or to taste)
- marjoram to taste (2-3 pinches) – optional

Method:

1. Soak casings to eliminate salt.
2. Place liver, bacon (skin removed) and meats in a big pot of water and cook until it's tender. It is better to bind the liver with a bit of twine onto the loop deal with of the container because liver will stick to bottom of the container.
3. In another container make the rice until soft. Drain and allow it to cool.
4. Inside a skillet, heat 2 tablespoons of lard and sauté the finely cut onions until smooth and somewhat caramelized.
5. After the liver, bacon and meats are prepared, slice them into chunks and grind them. Grind the sautéed onions as

well. Season the mixture with paprika, pepper and salt, and you'll then add marjoram too if you'd like. Blend them up with your hands until it is mixed thoroughly.

6. Stuff the casings loosely or the hurka will break up during cooking. Connect the ends of every link.

7. Place 1-2 or even more hurka in a colander (amount depends upon colander's size) and boil them for approx. for 2-3 minutes in gradually simmering water. Remove the hurka and drop into cool water immediately. Transfer them onto solid wood planks and let them dried out.

8. You can make hurka immediately or you can freeze them the next day.

Chapter Three: Hungarian Dinner Recipes

Vasi Pecsenye (Pork Roast Soaked in Garlic Milk)

Serves: 4

Ingredients:

- 4 fine slices of boneless pork butt or pork loin
- 4-5 garlic cloves
- 3-4 tablespoons flour
- 2 teaspoons paprika
- 1 cup milk
- oil or lard for frying
- salt and pepper to taste

Method:

1. Pound the slices very thin with a meat tenderizer. Cut 2-3 slits on the edges of each slice (since boneless pork butt and pork loin tend to curl when cooked at high heat, cutting the slits will prevent this from happening). Put them in a dish, add crushed garlic and pour milk to drown the slices. Put cover, place it in the fridge and let the meat soak in the milk overnight.
2. The following day drain the meat and discard the milk. Sprinkle both sides of the slices with salt and pepper. Mix flour and paprika, and coat the slices with this flour. In a large skillet, heat 1/2 inch of oil until hot. Add slices and fry them until both sides are crispy and golden. Place the slices on paper towel to drain excess oil.
3. Serve with steamed rice or crushed potatoes.

Körömpörkölt (Pig Feet Stew)

Serves: 2

Ingredients:

- 2 pig hind feet
- 4-5 medium-large potatoes
- 80 g (2 3/4 oz) smoked bacon
- 3 garlic cloves
- 2 teaspoon salt
- 1 bell or wax pepper
- 1 small tomato
- 1 big onion
- 1 heaping tbsp sweet paprika
- 1/2 teaspoon hot paprika
- 1/4 teaspoon caraway seeds

Method:

1. Prepare the feet, you can ask your butcher to cut up the feet. Wash and carefully clean them, eliminating hairs and brownish skin pieces.
2. Inside a container fry cut bacon until crispy. Add finely cut onion and garlic to the hot bacon excess fat and sauté until soft. Remove container from heat, add meat and paprika, and mix it. Pour in water, just enough to cover the meals and put the container back to stove. Add salt, caraway seeds, coarsely cut pepper and tomato. Cook with low heat for about 2-3 hours; cooking food time depends upon how old the pig was.
3. When cooking, if the liquid boils away, pour in more water, but only in small servings because the gravy should be solid by the end.
4. In the meantime, peel off and slice the potatoes into quarters. Once the meat is almost done, add potatoes to

the stew and cook until smooth and soft (bones can be easily removed). Or make them separately, in salty water.
5. Serve while hot, with white breads and pickles.

Tordai Pecsenye (Roast of Torda)

Serves: 6

Ingredients:

- 6 slices of pork (skin-on pork loin or pork blade steak – slices should be thicker)
- 500 ml (2 cups) water
- 30 g (2 tablespoons) untreated salt
- 1 small onion (peeled)
- 4 garlic cloves (peeled)
- 400-500 g (1 lb.) lard for frying

For the spicy potatoes:

- 800 g (1 3/4 lb.) small potatoes
- 300-400 g (3/4 lb.) lard or oil for frying
- 1 teaspoon salt
- 1-2 tablespoons corn flour
- 1/2 teaspoon paprika
- 1/4-1/4 teaspoon pepper, marjoram, thyme

Method:

1. Dissolve the salt in water. Cut 4-5 slits on the sides to avoid it from curling. Coating the pieces in a dish and put the brine over them. Make sure that the water addresses every cut. Chill for at least 3-4 hours.
2. Inside a deep-frying skillet, melt the lard. Add peeled garlic and onion cloves. After the lard is hot enough, remove onion and garlics and carefully place the pork pieces in to the lard. Fry over medium heat until soft and golden brownish. If they are done, move the pieces onto a dish lined with paper towel to remove the excess fat.
3. Peel off the potatoes and cut them into quarters. Cook them in salty water until about halfway done

(approximately 5-10 minutes). Drain and place them into a dish. Sprinkle and coating them equally with cornflour, season with salt, pepper, marjoram, paprika, and salt. Melt the lard on a frying skillet and fry the potatoes until brown and crispy. Use a slotted spoon to transfer them in paper towels to soak up excess lard.

4. Serve roast of Torda with spicy pickles and potatoes.

Csülök Pékné Módra (Braised and Roasted Pork Shank)

Serves: 6

Ingredients:

- 1 large or 2 small pork shanks (approx. 1,5 kg with bone)
- 1 kg potatoes
- 10 black pepper corns
- 5 allspice corns
- 4 teaspoon salt
- 4 garlic cloves
- 3 onions or 10 shallots
- 1 bay leaf
- 1 tablespoon oil
- 1 teaspoon caraway seeds

Method:

1. Place the pork shank in a big pot, add water, salt, bay leaf, peeled garlic cloves, dark pepper and allspice corns. Take it to a boil, and over low heat, cook for about 2-2,5 hours or until soft.
2. In the meantime, boil potatoes with their skin on in somewhat salted water until fifty percent done. Peel them, slice into quarters and place in a roasting skillet greased with oil.
3. Preheat the oven to 200 °C. Remove the shank from water and put on the potato bed. Add peeled shallots or sliced up onions and 1-2 ladles of the cooking food liquid, sprinkle salt and caraway seeds on the meats and vegetables. Put in place the oven and roast for approximately 30-35 minutes until it turns brownish.
4. Serve with pickles.

Stuffed Chicken Legs

Serves: 6

Ingredients:

- 6 chicken legs
- 100 g (3 1/2 oz) chicken livers
- 100 g (3 1/2 oz) mushrooms (finely diced)
- 100 ml (1/2 cup) milk
- 1 medium-large egg
- 1 slice of bread
- 1 medium-large onion (finely chopped)
- 30 g (1 oz) butter
- 2 tablespoons breadcrumbs
- 2-3 sprigs of parsley (finely chopped)
- salt and pepper to taste

Method:

1. Clean the chicken legs. Dry out the legs with paper towels, sprinkle salt and pepper.
2. Melt the butter in a nonstick skillet and sauté the onions until soft. Add diced mushrooms and a pinch of salt, and cook until mushrooms are soft and all the moisture gone. Set aside and allow it cool.
3. Clean the livers, discard sinews, and puree with a hand blender or scrape them with a blade. Soak the breads slice in milk, then press it out as well as you possibly can. Place the liver purée, egg, sautéed mushrooms and onion, soaked bread, cut parsley, breadcrumbs, 1/4 teaspoon of salt and pepper in a dish and mash them thoroughly.
4. Place your finger carefully between your meats and skin of every poultry leg to create a pocket. Fill up the pouches

equally with the stuffing mixture. Place the legs, packed sides up, within an oven handbag. Form any leftover stuffing into a ball or elongated form, and put it in the oven handbag. Bake at 180°C until chicken is prepared through, then increase the heat to 210°C and roast until it turns golden brown.

Hungarian Gizzard Stew

Serves: 3

Ingredients:

- 800 g (1 3/4 lbs.) gizzards (chicken or turkey)
- 2 handfuls of green peas
- 2 handfuls of mushrooms (sliced)
- 1 wax pepper in whole
- 1 small tomato in whole
- 3 garlic cloves (finely chopped)
- 3 teaspoons paprika
- 2 teaspoons salt
- 1 large onion (finely chopped)
- 1 1/2 tablespoons lard
- 1/2 teaspoon hot paprika
- 1/2 teaspoon black pepper

Method:

1. Wash and trim gizzards thoroughly.
2. In a deep skillet heat lard and sauté onions and garlic until translucent. Add gizzards and cook until they turn white. Remove from the heat, salt and pepper, sprinkle with paprika, and give it a good stir. Pour in enough water to cover most of the food. Add the wax pepper and tomato, and bring it to a boil. Decrease the heat, cover and slowly simmer. (Add enough water during to have enough gravy in the end.)
3. When gizzards are tender, add green peas and mushrooms and cook for further 5-10 minutes.
4. Serve hot with fries.

Borsos Tokány (Pepper Pork Ragout)

Serves: 4

Ingredients:

- 1 kg (2 lb.) boneless pork
- 100 ml (1/2 cup) water
- 70 g (2 1/2 oz) bacon (minced)
- 3 garlic cloves (finely minced)
- 2 teaspoon black pepper
- 2 tablespoons sour cream
- 1 onion (finely minced)
- 1 teaspoon salt
- 1 wax pepper, sliced
- 1 tomato (sliced)
- 1 tablespoon flour

Method:

1. In a non-stick pan fry the bacon until crispy.
2. Add finely chopped onions, wait for about 2-4 minutes then add finely chopped garlic and sauté in the bacon lard until soft.
3. Add the pork cubes and cook over medium heat. Add salt and pepper, and pour in enough water to cover three-quarters of the food.
4. Add sliced wax pepper and tomato, cover and slowly simmer. Add more water if necessary, tokány should have a nice sauce.
5. Meanwhile whisk together flour, sour cream and 100 ml/ 1/2 cup of water. When the meat is soft and tender, stir the sour cream thickener into the ragout. Modify the salt and pepper, and cook for about 1-2 minutes.
6. Serve with noodles or wam rice.

Hungarian Noodles

Serves: 4

Ingredients:

- 16 ounces noodles (cooked and drained)
- 1 can condensed cream of mushroom soup
- 3 chicken bouillon cubes
- 2 cups cottage cheese
- 2 cups sour cream
- 2 tablespoons Worcestershire sauce
- 2 tablespoons poppy seeds
- 2 cloves garlic (minced)
- 1 sliced mushroom (small package)
- 1/2 cup chopped onion
- 1/4 cup boiling water
- 1/4 teaspoon hot chili sauce
- 1/4 cup shredded parmesan cheese
- medium – large paprika

Method:

1. In a large bowl, dissolve bouillon in water. Add all of the ingredients, stir in cottage cheese, sour cream and noodles, mix thoroughly.
2. Pour into a greased 2 1/2-quart baking dish. Sprinkle with the Parmesan cheese and paprika.
3. Put cover and bake at 350 degrees for about 45 minutes or until heated through.

Sárgaborsó Főzelék (Yellow Split Pea Stew)

Serves: 4

Ingredients:

- 250 g (8-9 oz) yellow split peas
- 2 heaping tablespoons flour
- 2 tablespoons sour cream
- 2 garlic cloves (minced)
- 1 onion (minced)
- 1 tablespoon lard
- 1 bay leaf
- 1 tablespoon homemade seasoning
- 1/2 teaspoon paprika
- 1/4 tablespoon ground black pepper
- salt and pepper to taste

Method:

1. Pick through the peas and remove any debris and dirt. Pour a little bit of water to cover the split peas and leave them on the counter overnight.
2. The next day, drain and rinse the split peas. Melt the lard and sauté the finely chopped onion and garlic until translucent. Pour in 1 liter/4 cups of water and add the split peas. Add homemade seasoning, bay leaf, paprika and pepper, cover and cook over medium heat until soft.
3. Once the peas are tender, whisk flour, sour cream and 100 ml / 1/2 cup of water together and in a fine stream pour into the soup while stirring constantly. Modify salt and pepper, cook for a few minutes until the stew thickens.
4. Split pea stew goes well with roasted sausages or Vienna sausages.

Fasírozott (Hungarian Pork Patties)

Serves: 6

Ingredients:

- 500 g (1 lb.) minced pork
- 3 medium – large eggs
- 2 garlic cloves
- 2 teaspoons salt
- 2 teaspoons sweet ground paprika
- 1 cup bread crumbs
- 1/2 teaspoon pepper
- small bunch of parsley leaves (finely minced)
- oil or lard for frying

Method:

1. Place the minced pork in a bowl. Add the eggs, bread crumbs and crushed garlic.
2. Season with salt, pepper and paprika, lastly, add finely chopped parsley.
3. Mix until well combined.
4. Form tiny balls with your hands.
5. In a frying pan heat up oil or lard and slowly fry patties in batches on both sides until golden brown.
6. Serve with hot rice or fries.

Chicken Paprikash With Buttered Macaroni

Serves: 6

Ingredients:

- 2 pounds boneless chicken thighs (skinless and, cut into 1cm strips)
- 4 ounces chorizo (diced)
- 4 1/2 tablespoons soured cream
- 3 1/3 cups plum tomatoes
- 3 tablespoons paprika
- 3 tablespoons flat leaf parsley (chopped)
- 3 cups macaroni
- 2 1/8 tablespoons butter (room temperature)
- 2 cups chicken stock
- 2 tablespoons flour
- 1 1/2 large onion (cut in half and finely sliced)
- 1 1/2 red pepper (cut into thin strips)
- 1 1/2 large garlic clove (finely chopped)
- 1 1/2 teaspoons cayenne pepper

Method:

1. Heat a large, deep frying pan over medium-high heat and fry the chorizo for 5 minutes until crisp, stirring often. Remove on to a plate with a slotted spoon. Add the chicken and cook for about 5 minutes, until browned all over. Put it aside with the chorizo.
2. Add the onion and red pepper, and cook over a medium-low heat for about 10-15 minutes, until the onions and peppers have softened. Add the garlic, paprika and cayenne pepper for the final minute of cooking.
3. Add the chicken and chorizo back into the pan with the tomatoes and chicken stock. Crush the tomatoes with a fork to break them up a little and season the paprikash

lightly. Bring to a boil, then simmer for 15-20 minutes until the sauce has reduced.

4. In a small bowl, combine the flour and 10g butter into a paste. Stir this into the sauce and simmer for 1-2 minutes, until the sauce has thickened. Stir in the soured cream and scatter over the parsley.

5. While the chicken is simmering, cook the macaroni according to the instructions on the packet. Drain well, then add it back to the pan with the remaining 10g butter and stir, until the butter has melted. Serve the chicken with the buttered macaroni.

Vegan Hungarian Goulash with Tofu and Potato

Serves: 4

Ingredients:

- 700 grams tofu (firm, cubed, approx. two packages)
- 2 pounds baby red potatoes (cut in half)
- 5 ounces tomato paste
- 5 cloves garlic (grated)
- 5 tablespoons paprika (hot or mild, your choice)
- 3 cups water
- 1 medium-large onion (finely diced)
- 1 teaspoon olive oil
- 1 teaspoon dried oregano
- 1 teaspoon dried basil
- 1 whole bay leaf
- 1/2 teaspoon salt
- 1/2 teaspoon ground black pepper
- 1/4 cup fresh parsley (chopped, and for garnish)

Method:

1. Start by cooking the onions in the olive oil over medium heat. Use a large pot – a Dutch oven is perfect for this recipe.
2. Once the onions are cooked, add in the garlic and stir through – cook for 1 minute.
3. Add in the tomato paste, paprika, salt, black pepper, oregano, basil, and bay leaf. Stir these ingredients into the onions and garlic. Allow the spices and the tomato paste to cook for 2-3 minutes.
4. Add in the potatoes and the water. Stir to combine.
5. Place a lid on the pot and cook for 5 minutes.

6. Reduce heat to simmer, add the tofu and stir to combine. Be careful not to break up the tofu pieces. Try to keep the tofu into solid, uniform chunks. I found that using a silicone spoon worked well.
7. Continue to simmer for 30 minutes. The sauce will thicken and the potatoes will finish cooking. Once the potatoes are cooked, stir in the parsley and turn off the heat.
8. Allow the goulash to sit for 5 minutes undisturbed before serving.

Creamy Mushroom Paprikash Over Pasta

Serves: 4

Ingredients:

- 1 lb. cremini mushrooms (quartered)
- 3 tablespoons unsalted butter
- 2 cups yellow onion (thinly sliced)
- 2 tablespoons tomato paste
- 1 teaspoon sweet Hungarian paprika
- 3/4 cup dry white wine (6 fl. oz./180 ml)
- 3/4-pound fresh pappardelle
- 1/2 cup sour cream (4 fl. oz./125 ml, or crème fraîche)
- 1/2 teaspoon caraway seeds
- 1/4 cup fresh dill (minced)
- salt and ground pepper to taste

Method:

1. Bring a large pot of salted water to a boil. Meanwhile, in a wide fry pan over medium heat, melt 2 Tbs. of the butter. Add the mushrooms, caraway seeds and 1/2 tsp. salt, and sauté until the mushrooms release their liquid and begin to brown, 8 minutes.
2. Add the onion and sauté until the onion is tender and browned, 5 minutes. Stir in the tomato paste and paprika and cook for 1 minute. Reduce the heat to medium, add the wine and simmer until about half the liquid has evaporated and the sauce has thickened, 2 minutes. Cover and set aside.
3. Add the pasta to the boiling water and cook until al dente according to the package instructions. Reserve 1/2 cup (4 fl. oz./125 ml) of the cooking liquid and drain the pasta. Place the pasta in a large serving bowl and toss with the

remaining 1 Tbs. butter. Fold the sour cream and dill into the mushroom sauce and season to taste with salt and pepper, adding a bit of the pasta cooking liquid to moisten, if necessary.

4. Spoon the sauce over the pasta and serve immediately.

Hungarian Braised Beef

Serves: 6

Ingredients:

- 3 pounds chuck roast (cut into cubes)
- 10 3/4 ounces tomato puree
- 6 tablespoons sweet Hungarian paprika
- 4 tablespoons tomato paste
- 4 cloves garlic (chopped)
- 3 tablespoons olive oil
- 2 tablespoons Worcestershire sauce
- 1 medium-large onion (finely diced)
- 3/4 cup red wine (not overly dry)
- 1 cup beef broth
- salt and pepper to taste

Method:

5. Salt and pepper beef chunks, and sprinkle with Worcestershire. Working in batches so beef is not crowded, brown in olive oil in heavy pot. Make sure it gets a good, brown sear on all sides. Remove to a bowl or baking sheet.
6. Reduce heat to medium and add onions; when they are softened and beginning to color, add garlic and sauté for a minute or two (do not allow to brown). Deglaze pan with red wine and allow wine to reduce by 1/2.
7. Dust beef chunks with paprika, making sure all sides are covered; rub it in to be sure all the paprika adheres. Use the entire six tablespoons, even though that looks like a tremendous amount of paprika.
8. Add tomato puree to pot and stir to combine with onion/wine mixture. Return beef chunks to pot in a

single layer, if possible. Add enough beef stock so liquid is even with top of beef chunks.

9. Lower heat to low, cover, and simmer for 2 1/2 hours, checking frequently to see if more broth is needed. Liquid level should stay within 1/2 inch of top of beef.

10. Stir tomato paste into sauce, uncover, and continue to cook for 30 minutes, or until beef is fork-tender. Serve over rice or egg noodles.

Parrag's Hungarian Pork Stew and Nokedli Pasta

Serves: 8

Ingredients:

- 9 3/4-inch thick boneless center cut loin pork chops, trimmed the fat off, sliced in half length-wise, pounded 1/4 inch thin (if you can find thin loin chops, you'll only have to pound them thin)
- 8 medium-large yellow onions (cut into cubes)
- 6-8 cups water (or enough water enough to fully immerse all the ingredients)
- 3 tablespoons sweet Hungarian paprika
- 1/3 cup canola/vegetable oil plus more for frying
- 1 tablespoon salt
- 1 tablespoon pepper
- flour for dredging
- Vegeta to taste (approx. 1 tablespoon). Or you can use vegetable/chicken soup seasoning packets
- 1 cup sour cream

Method:

1. In a large pot (6 qt) over medium to medium-high heat, add onions and canola oil. Sauté onions until they are translucent, but not browned. Add more oil when necessary to keep them slick in the process. When the onions have finished cooking, turn down heat to low, add paprika to mixture and stir to mix well.
2. While the onions are cooking, season each side of the pork slices generously with salt and pepper. Dredge the slices in flour on each side.
3. In a frying pan over medium-high to high heat, heat about an inch of canola or vegetable oil. Fry each slice of pork until just barely golden brown around the edges,

about 1-2 minutes, flipping halfway through. If they are thin enough, this will be enough to cook them fully. Lay them between sheets of paper towel on a plate to catch excess oil.

4. Cut each of the pork slices in half and place them back in the pot with the onions. Add enough water to the pot to cover the pork and onions. Cover pot and simmer on medium heat for 45 minutes to 1 hour. Stir occasionally.

5. When the stew is thickened up a bit from the flour and the onions are starting to disappear, it is ready for the final seasoning. Add salt, pepper and Vegeta seasoning to taste. Add sour cream and stir until the stew is a rich, thick consistency.

For the Nokedli Pasta:

Ingredients:

- 4 cups all-purpose flour
- 2 eggs
- 1 teaspoon salt
- large pot filled halfway with salted, boiling water

Method:

1. In a large mixing bowl, add eggs and flour and a bit of the water. Stir until the consistency is like a very dry dough. Add water gradually, and stir between each addition to ensure no lumps have formed. You're going for pancake batter consistency and if you do it slowly gradually like this, there will be hardly any lumps.

2. Using a nokedli maker, drop the batter on top and push it through into the pot of boiling water. It will sink initially. When the batter floats to the surface, about 30 seconds, it has finished cooking. With a slotted spoon, scoop out the pasta and place in a large bowl. Add a bit of

canola oil and stir once all the pasta is finished to prevent it from sticking together.

Hungarian Wiener Schnitzel

Serves: 4

Ingredients:

- veal cutlets
- 3 eggs
- flour
- seasoned bread crumbs
- butter
- olive oil
- salt and pepper to taste

Method:

1. Place a large pan over medium heat.
2. Place the veal or turkey cutlets between two pieces of wax paper and use a meat tenderizer (any large can or bottle will do) to pound the cutlets until they are roughly ¼-inch thick.
3. Now that the pan is warm, add enough olive oil and butter to coat the bottom of the pan.
4. Set up an assembly station with three parts: a plate for the flour, a dish for the eggs (beaten together) and a plate for the bread crumbs.
5. Dredge each cutlet first in the flour, then the eggs and finally the bread crumbs.
6. Place the coated cutlets into the pan of melted butter and oil and sauté on both sides for 4 minutes, or until the bread crumbs are golden brown and the meat is fully cooked.
7. Serve with a slice of lemon and salt and pepper to taste.

Hungarian Brisket

Serves: 6

Ingredients:

- 1 beef brisket (4 to 5-pound, cut in half)
- 8 ounces tomato sauce
- 4 large vidalia onions (sliced)
- 2 tablespoons Hungarian paprika
- 1 1/2 teaspoons garlic salt (divided)
- 1 teaspoon fresh ground black pepper (divided)
- 1 tablespoon all-purpose flour
- 1/2 cup canola oil
- 3/8 oz beef bouillon cube (large)
- 1/2 cup water

Method:

1. Heat oil in a large Dutch oven over medium-high heat; add onions. Cook, stirring often, 25 to 30 minutes or until onions are golden brown and caramelized. Stir in 1 teaspoon garlic salt and 1/2 teaspoon pepper. Remove onions from pan with a slotted spoon, reserving oil in pan.
2. Sprinkle flour, paprika, and remaining 1/2 teaspoon each garlic salt and pepper on all sides of brisket. Heat reserved oil in Dutch oven over medium-high heat. Sear brisket 2 to 3 minutes on each side or until lightly browned.
3. Combine beef bouillon cube and 1/2 cup water, stirring until bouillon is dissolved. Pour over brisket halves. Add onions and tomato sauce; bring to a boil. Cover, reduce heat, and simmer 2 1/2 hours.
4. Remove brisket from Dutch oven, and place on a large, rimmed baking sheet or platter. Place another baking sheet on top of brisket; place a heavy skillet or large cans

on top of baking sheet. (Weighing down the cooked brisket improves texture and makes slicing easier the next day.) Refrigerate brisket overnight. In a separate container, cover and refrigerate onions and pan juices.

5. Skim fat from onion-tomato mixture; discard fat. Heat mixture in Dutch oven over medium-low heat. Slice brisket across grain into thin slices. Add brisket to pan, and cook 10 minutes or until thoroughly heated.

Note:

- The grain in brisket often changes while slicing, so continually reposition the brisket and slice against the grain.

Hungarian Stuffed Peppers

Serves: 4

Ingredients:

- 5 green bell peppers
- 29 ounces canned diced tomatoes (with their juice)
- 2 pounds ripe tomatoes (peeled and diced)
- 2 tablespoons tomato paste
- 2/3 long-grain cup rice (rinsed and drained)
- 2 tablespoons brown sugar (or to taste)
- 2 tablespoons fresh lemon juice (strained, or to taste)
- 1 slice challah bread (day-old or stale)
- 1 medium-large onion
- 1 teaspoon paprika (optional)
- 1 bay leaf (optional)
- 1/2 cup water
- 1/2-pound ground beef
- 1/4 cup fresh parsley (chopped)
- freshly ground pepper
- salt and pepper to taste

Method:

1. Slice half the onion and put it in a stew pan. Add tomatoes, tomato paste, water, bay leaf and a pinch of salt and pepper. Mix well and bring to a boil. Cover and cook over low heat for 15 minutes.
2. Boil rice in a saucepan with two cups boiling salted water for 10 minutes. Rinse with cold water and drain well.
3. Soak bread in cold water and squeeze dry. Put in a bowl. Coarsely grate remaining onion half and add to bowl. Add beef, parsley, paprika, one-half teaspoon salt and

one-quarter to one-half teaspoon pepper and mix well. Add rice and mix again.

4. Cut a slice off top (stem end) of each pepper. Reserve slice; remove stem, core and seeds from each pepper. Spoon stuffing into whole peppers and cover with reserved slices. Stand them up in tomato sauce. Cover and simmer, adding boiling water from time to time if sauce becomes too thick. Cook 45 minutes to one hour, or until peppers are very tender. Gently remove peppers. Discard bay leaf.

5. If the sauce is too thin, cook it, uncovered, over medium-high heat, stirring often, until thickened. Add sugar and simmer for one minute. Add lemon juice. Adjust seasoning. Serve peppers hot, with sauce.

Csirkepörkölt (Hungarian Chicken Stew)

Serves: 4

Ingredients:

- 1 1/4 pounds boneless, skinless chicken breasts (cut into small pieces)
- 2 tablespoons pork fat
- 2 garlic cloves (minced)
- 1 medium onion (chopped)
- 1 tablespoon paprika
- 1 medium-large tomato (chopped)
- 1 red bell pepper (chopped)
- 1/2 cup water
- 2 teaspoons sea salt

Method:

1. In a deep pan, heat the pork fat over medium heat. Once heated, add the onion and cook, stirring occasionally, until softened. Stir in the garlic and cook until just fragrant, about 30 seconds.
2. Remove the pot from heat and stir in the paprika. Add the chicken pieces and return the pot to medium heat. Cook, stirring occasionally, until the edges of the chicken are browned. Mix in the tomato, bell pepper, and 1/2 cup water. Season with salt.
3. Once the liquid comes to a boil, reduce heat to a simmer, cover, and cook for an hour, until the chicken is cooked through and tender.
4. Season with additional salt if needed.

Paprikash Chicken Stroganoff

Serves: 5

Ingredients:

- 1 pound boneless and skinless chicken breasts
- 8 ounces white button mushrooms (sliced and diced)
- 2 tablespoons all-purpose flour
- 2 tablespoons olive oil
- 2 tablespoons tomato paste
- 3 cloves garlic (finely chopped)
- 1 tablespoon smoked paprika
- 1 teaspoon salt
- 1 tablespoon butter
- 1 medium-large yellow onion (chopped)
- 1 3/4 cups low sodium chicken broth
- 1 bay leaf
- 1/2 teaspoon black pepper
- 1/4 cup plain yogurt (creme fraiche, or sour cream)
- chopped fresh parsley (garnish)

Method:

1. In a medium bowl toss the cubed chicken with the paprika, salt and pepper. Sprinkle the flour on top of the chicken and toss to coat.
2. Heat the olive oil in a large nonstick skillet over medium heat until hot. Add the chicken in a single layer and cook until golden brown on each side, tossing occasionally, about 5 minutes. Don't worry if the chicken is not cooked through, it will fully cook later on in the sauce. Scrape the chicken onto a plate and set aside.
3. Add the butter to the pan, and stir in the onions and mushrooms. Saute the mixture, stirring occasionally and

scraping up the browned bits from the chicken, until the onion is translucent and the onions and mushrooms are browned, about 5 minutes. Add the garlic and cook for another minute, until fragrant.

4. Pour in about 1/4 cup of the chicken broth and deglaze the pan by scraping up any bits from the bottom. Stir in the tomato paste, whisking to combine. Add the rest of the chicken broth and the bay leaf, stirring well.

5. Add the chicken back into the skillet and simmer the mixture over medium-low to medium heat, until the chicken is cooked through and the sauce thickens slightly, about 5-6 minutes. Stir in the yogurt (or creme fraiche or sour cream) and cook for about 2-3 minutes longer. I used sour cream in mine. Let the mixture simmer for 2-3 minutes until thickened. Serve over mashed potatoes, egg noodles or rice and garnish with fresh parsley, if desired.

Chapter Four: Hungarian Dessert Recipes

Rózsafánk (Rose Doughnuts)

Serves: 3

Ingredients:

- 400 g (3 1/4 cups) flour
- 80 g (1/3 cup) butter
- 5-6 tablespoons sour cream
- 4 egg yolks
- 2 tablespoons rum
- 2 tablespoons sugar
- 1 egg white for sticking the circles
- pinch of salt
- lard or oil for deep-frying

Method:

1. Rub in butter and flour. Add egg yolks, sugar, salt, rum and sour cream, and knead until smooth and pliable. Wrap the dough and put in the refrigerator for 30 minutes.
2. On a floured surface roll out the dough to a thickness of 2 milimeters. Cut out rounds using 3 cutters of different size. With a knife cut the edges of each round. Spread the middle of the biggest circle with slightly beaten egg white, then place a middle-sized round on top.
3. Spread egg white on the centre, put on the smallest round and gently press together.
4. Fry the doughnuts until golden. Place them on paper towel to absorb oil.
5. Serve warm with jam.

Őznyelv (Deer's Tongue)

Serves: 4

Ingredients:

- 500 g (1 lb.) puff pastry
- 150 g (5 1/3 oz) sweet dark chocolate (or to your liking)
- 150 g (2/3 cup) whipping cream
- 100 g (3/4 cup) powdered sugar for rolling out the dough
- 50 g (3 1/2 tablespoons) butter

Method:

1. Heat the cream and pour over the chocolate broken into small pieces. Stir until chocolate melts completely, then add butter and keep stirring until butter is fully incorporated. Set the chocolate filling aside and let it cool.
2. Preheat the oven to 200°C. Line two baking trays with parchment paper.
3. Dust a pastry board with powdered sugar and roll out puff pastry until 5 mm/ 1/5 inch thick. Cut out circles with a 5 cm/2-inch cutter. Roll out each circle into an oval shape. Place the ovals on the prepared baking trays and poke them with a fork. Bake them for 8-10 minutes or until golden brown.
4. Once the cookies are cool, spread half of them with the filling and top with remaining cookies to make sandwiches.

Hungarian Cake

Serves: 4

Ingredients:

Dough:

- 600 g flour
- 140 g margarine or butter
- 8 tablespoons sour cream (or you can use plain yogurt or buttermilk)
- 1 teaspoon baking powder
- 2 eggs
- 200 g sugar

Chocolate-rum cream:

- 400 g sugar
- 100 g dark chocolate
- 100 g milk chocolate
- 20 tablespoons flour
- 3 tablespoons cocoa
- 3 tablespoons of rum
- 2 L of milk
- 1 vanilla sugar

Chocolate-rum cream:

- 150 g dark chocolate
- 100 g milk chocolate
- 1 tablespoon sugar
- approx. 3-4 tablespoons milk (add more if you think the glaze is not smooth, but don't make it too liquid)

Method:

1. Pour flour mixed with baking powder on the table and chop with margarine. Add sugar, eggs, sour cream and knead the dough. Then divide the dough into 6 equal parts. roll the dough into a rectangle that is the size of a baking pan (32x33 cm). Bake on the reverse side of the pan.

2. For the cream, you need two bowls. Place 1500 ml milk in a saucepan over low heat and in the remaining 500 ml milk mix flour and sugar. When the milk starts to boil, add the mixture and stir well until it's cooked. Remove cream from heat and add chocolate, vanilla sugar and rum.

3. When the first layer of cake is baked, start making the cream. It is important that hot cream goes on hot layers, so that cake is moist and soft right away. So you put the first layer, cream it, second layer - cream. And you repeat till the end. The last layer shouldn't be creamed, because on top we will put chocolate glaze.

4. Melt it in a saucepan and pour on top of the cake. Working quickly, use a knife or long spatula to smooth the glaze across the cake letting it fall over the sides. When the glazing is completed, let the cake cool on the counter or in the refrigerator until the glaze has solidified.

Hungarian Kurtos Kalacs (Chimney Cake)

Serves: 6

Ingredients:

- 500 gr plain flour
- 200 ml full-fat milk
- 5 tablespoons vegetable oil
- 3 tablespoons regular sugar
- 2 tablespoons yeast (approx. 14 grams)
- 2 eggs
- Cinnamon powder
- sprinkle of salt to taste

Method:

Preparing the dough:

1. Warm the milk in the small saucepan over medium-low heat. combine the warm milk, sugar, and yeast into the big bowl and give it a good stir. Set aside for 5 minutes or until a thick bubbly foam has formed on top of the milk. combine flour and salt in the stand mixer's bowl. Make a hole in the center and pour in vegetable oil, two eggs, and the milk mixture.
2. Mix using the medium setting for about 5 to 10 minutes, depending on your stand mixer. Our Kitchen aid stand mixer only took 5 minutes. The chimney cake dough is ready when the dough has become a solid mass and does not stick to your hands. Don't add in extra flour if you notice that the dough is too sticky, add in a few more drops of vegetable oil instead. Cover with cling film and set aside to rest for 1 hour, or doubled in size.
3. Use this time to create the holders. We tried keeping this as simple as possible by using one or two paper towel

tubes. Wrap them tightly in tin foil, fold the remaining tin foil inwards. Test it on the baking tray to see if it aligns, and stays put. We're going to wrap the dough over these holders in the next part. Since these chimney cakes need to be heated all the way around and inside, these make-shift holders will do perfectly fine.

Baking the chimney cakes:

1. When the kurtos kalac dough has doubled in size, place it on a clean working surface. Don't sprinkle your counter top with flour beforehand. knead the dough until smooth, then divide into six portions. Roll each portion into a long string and roll it onto the prepared holder. The thicker these strings are, the softer they will be eventually. Test a few out to see which thickness you prefer.

2. Pre-heat your oven to a temperature of 200 degrees Celsius, or 392 degrees Fahrenheit. Sprinkle each kurtos kalac with sugar and/or cinnamon. Place each holder on the edges of your baking tray, and bake them for about 10 to 15 minutes. Roll each holder once in a while, so that the crust color is evenly browned.

3. When done baking, it's best to eat the chimney cakes immediately. But you can store these for up to two days when wrapped in cling film.

Hungarian Jam Squares

Serves: 15

Ingredients:

- 2 3/4 cups all-purpose flour
- 2 medium-large eggs (lightly beaten)
- 2 teaspoons pure vanilla extract
- 1 cup granulated sugar
- 1 teaspoon baking powder
- 1 cup cold unsalted butter (cut into cubes)
- 1-quart jam (any flavor to your liking)
- powdered sugar (to dust the cookies)
- 1/2 teaspoon salt

Method:

1. Preheat oven to 325 F. Apply a 15" x 10" jelly move pan (with edges) with cooking food aerosol and then collection the bottom or more both of the edges with parchment paper. (to help remove cookies when done)
2. In large capacity food processor, with knife attached, add the flour, sugars, baking salt and powder. Pulse several times to combine.
3. Add butter and process until butter integrated in to the flour.
4. Add vanilla to the eggs, even though the processor is operating, pour in to the flour/butter combination and process until an easy dough. If it appears too sticky, put in a bit more flour. (you ought to be able to pick and choose it up and form it into a ball)
5. Reserve 1/4 of dough and press the rest of the dough in to the bottom level and edges of the ready skillet. Pass on the jam equally on the dough.
6. With remaining fifty percent of dough, move or press out into a rectangle, about 1/8 in. solid and slice into strips.

Arrange dough strips within the jam in a crisscross pattern. (you certainly do not need to lattice them, just make sure they are crisscross combination, by establishing all the strips in a single path on the jam, and then go the other way with the others) Press the sides to seal.

7. Bake in the oven until gently brownish on the sides, about 25 -30 minutes. Remove from oven and cool completely before trimming into squares. Dirt with powdered glucose, if desired.

Hungarian Varga Beles (Noodle Cake)

Serves: 4

Ingredients:

- 1 kg fresh white cheese
- 8 medium-large eggs
- 800 grams noodles (or ribbon pasta)
- 400 gr sugar
- 200 gr raisins
- 1 lemon
- 1 tablespoon vanilla sugar

Method:

1. First boil the noodles in salted water, as you usually boil the noodles or pasta. Then, beat the eggs just like you beat them for scrambled eggs. Then mingle well with all the ingredients, including the noodles (after they`re boiled and cooled).
2. Put the composition in a tray. Use some baking paper so the cake doesn`t stick to the bottom of the tray. Put it in the oven for about 20-30 minutes on medium temperature.

Authentic Hungarian Pinwheels

Serves: 10

Ingredients:

- 8 ounces softened full-fat cream cheese
- 1 medium-large egg (plus 1 tablespoon water for egg wash)
- 1 cup all-purpose flour
- 1/2 cup softened salted butter
- 1/2 cup strawberry jam (or filling of your choice)

Method:

1. Preheat oven to 350° F and line a baking sheet with parchment paper or a silicone baking mat.
2. In the bowl of a stand mixer, mix together the cream cheese and butter and whip until combined, about 2-3 minutes. Add in the flour and stir until a loose dough has formed.
3. Dump the mixture out onto a floured work surface and gently knead the dough until a cohesive dough forms. Roll it out into a ¼-inch thick rectangle and cut into 3x3 inch squares using a ravioli cutter.
4. Transfer the dough to the prepared baking sheet carefully. Using the ravioli cutter, cut the dough diagonally from each corner ¾ of the way to the center. Repeat with all squares of dough. Place 1 tablespoon of jam in the center of each pinwheel.
5. Fold each corner towards the center of the pastry, using the pictures above as a guide. Lightly brush the pastries with the prepared egg wash.
6. Place the pan in the oven and bake for 20 minutes, or until lightly browned. Let cool for 10 minutes before serving.

Hungarian Dobosh Torte

Serves: 16

Ingredients:

For the Cake:

- 4 medium-large eggs (slightly beaten)
- 8 ounces softened unsalted butter
- 1 cup sugar
- 1 teaspoon vanilla
- 1 1/2 cups all-purpose flour

For the filling:

- 5 medium-large egg whites
- 8 ounces sweet chocolate (chopped)
- 2 ounces unsweetened chocolate (chopped)
- 1-pound softened unsalted butter
- 1 cup sugar

For the caramel glaze:

- 2/3 cup sugar
- 1/3 cup water

Method:

The cake:

1. Heat oven to 350 F. In a large bowl, cream 8 ounces butter and 1 cup sugar until light and fluffy. Beat in 4 eggs, one at a time, then flour and vanilla until smooth.
2. Lightly coat the bottom of 7 (9-inch) round pans or bake as many layers at a time as you have 9-inch cake pans and reuse them to bake the rest of the batter with cooking spray.

3. Weigh the batter remembering to subtract for the weight of the bowl. Divide that number by 7 and that's how many ounces you will need for each pan in order to create even layers.
4. Bake for 7 minutes or until edges are very lightly brown. Don't overbake. Remove from oven, loosen layer and immediately invert onto a cake rack. Continue until all the batter is used.

The filling:

1. Melt both chocolates in a microwave and set aside to cool. In a large bowl, beat 1 pound butter on low for 2 minutes, then on medium for 3 minutes and finally on high for 5 minutes.
2. Place 5 egg whites and 1 cup sugar in a double boiler over medium heat. Whisk gently to 120 F. Transfer to a mixing bowl and whip on high until stiff peaks form.
3. Fold the melted and cooled chocolate into the butter, then fold in the egg whites until all traces of white are gone. Refrigerate until ready to use.

The caramel glaze:

1. Place 1 cake layer on a cake rack set over a pan to catch the drips. Mix 2/3 cup sugar and 1/3 cup water in a small heavy saucepan.
2. Without stirring, cook until sugar dissolves, comes to a boil and begins to darken in color. Swirling the pan, continue to boil until caramel becomes a golden brown.
3. Immediately pour caramel over the cake layer. With a buttered knife, quickly mark the glaze before it hardens into 16 equal wedges without cutting all the way through.

Assemble the Torte:

1. Place 1 cake layer on a serving plate, or in a 9-inch springform pan to use as a guide, and spread on 1/8-inch of filling.
2. Repeat with remaining layers and portions of filling, and finish with the glazed layer on top.
3. Use the rest of the filling to cover the sides of the cake. Sprinkle with ground nuts of choice, if desired. Refrigerate.
4. To serve, slice along the lines marked in the caramel glaze.

Madártej (Hungarian Floating Islands)

Serves: 4

Ingredients:

- 5 medium-large egg (separate the yolks and the whites)
- 2 cups whole milk
- 2 tablespoons vanilla sugar (or 2 tablespoons pure vanilla extract)
- 1 tablespoon sugar
- 1/4 cup sugar
- 1/2 vanilla bean (cut lengthwise)
- 1 tablespoon flour (optional)

Method:

1. In a large saucepan, bring water to boil.
2. Turn the heat down to slow simmer.
3. Beat the egg whites until stiff peaks form.
4. Beat in 1 Tbsp of sugar.
5. With a wooden spoon drop 2-3 spoonfuls of beaten egg whites into the simmering water.
6. In a few seconds the meringues will puff up, gently turn them over with the wooden spoon.
7. Cook the meringues for a few seconds longer and then transfer them with a slotted spoon to a serving bowl.
8. Beat the egg yolks and sugar for 3-4 minutes until very thick and creamy.
9. Add 1 Tbsp of flour and whisk to combine. This step is optional.
10. Add the milk and whisk to combine.
11. Transfer yolk-milk mixture to a saucepan.
12. Split the vanilla bean and add to the saucepan.
13. Slowly heat the mixture and keep stirring with a wooden spoon

14. You must NOT let the milk boil or the yolks will curdle. Let it come no higher than 175F or 80C. Dip the wooden spoon into the custard and run your finger along the back of the spoon. If the streak remains without the cream running down through the streak, it is ready.
15. If you use vanilla extract or vanilla sugar, now is the time to add to the hot custard.
16. Strain the hot custard through a fine sieve into a bowl.
17. If you used vanilla bean scrape the seeds into the hot custard and stir.
18. Pour the custard over the meringues.
19. Serve hot or chilled.

Hungarian Cookie Treasures

Serves: 12

Ingredients:

- 5 cups all-purpose flour
- 1 1/2 cups jam (or preserves of your choice, you can also use a nut filling)
- 1-pound softened real butter
- 1 cup granulated sugar
- 1 cup powdered sugar (for dusting)

Method:

1. With using a stand mixer, add the cream cheese, softened butter, and the 1 cup of granulated sugar. Mix on medium speed until well blended. If using honey, mix well with the goat cheese until smooth.
2. Add the flour one cup at a time, mixing until evenly incorporated. Remove dough from mixer and press it into a ball. Wrap in plastic and allow to rest in the refrigerator for 1 hour.
3. Preheat the oven to 375 degrees.
4. Sprinkle some powdered sugar on a smooth countertop or pastry board and roll dough out to approx. 1/4-inch-thick sheets. Cut the dough into 2-inch circles. Re-roll excess dough as needed.
5. Place 1 teaspoonful of jam or preserves in the center of circle.
6. Wet the cookie edges around the jam or preserves with your finger. Then place a second circle over the jam or preserves and firmly press down around the edges to encompass the jam or preserves. Take a fork and go all around the edge to seal jam or preserves in tightly (like you would for a pie crust). Repeat this process until you have used up all the dough.

7. Place the cookies on a baking sheet lined with parchment paper and bake for 8-10 minutes or until cookies begin to brown.
8. Remove from oven and place onto cookie rack.
9. If desired, dust cookies with powdered sugar.
10. These cookies keep well in the freezer for long-term storage. However, they should be stored in an airtight container in the refrigerator when completely cooled.

Diotorta (Hungarian Walnut Cake)

Serves: 4

Ingredients:

- 6 medium-large eggs (separate the whites and the yolks)
- 300 ml milk
- 300 grams butter (room temperature)
- 200 grams sugar
- 110 grams flour
- 6 tablespoons flour
- 4 tablespoons ground walnuts
- 3 1/2 tablespoons rum
- 3 tablespoons rum
- 1/2 cup ground walnuts (extra for garnish)
- 1 tablespoon vanilla extract

Method:

1. Preheat the oven to 180 degrees Celsius.
2. Beat the egg yolks with 40 grams sugar until pale and fluffy. Add the flour, walnuts, and rum.
3. Beat the egg whites with the rest of the sugar, then divided into 3 parts: 1 part at the beginning, another once they look whiter, and the rest when they are almost ready. Beat until firm peaks are formed.
4. Fold the egg whites into the egg yolk mixture, being careful not to over-beat.
5. Pour into a 22-centimeter cake mold lined with parchment. Bake for 30 to 35 minutes. Let it cool.
6. Cut horizontally into 3 layers. Set aside.
7. Dissolve the flour in the milk and bring to a boil in a heavy-bottomed pan, stirring until it thickens. Remove from the stove and set aside while it cools.

8. Using an electric mixer, cream the butter and sugar. Add the milk and flour mixture, walnuts, rum, and vanilla. Beat until creamy.
9. To assemble the cake, plate the first layer of sponge cake, spread some of the frosting on top. Add the second layer and more frosting, then add the top layer and cover the entire surface of the cake with the frosting. Sprinkle the rest of the walnuts on the sides of the cake.
10. Refrigerate for 24 hours before serving.

Szilvás Gombóc (Hungarian Plum Dumplings)

Serves: 15

Ingredients:

- 14 ounces flour
- 15 tablespoons butter
- 15 tablespoons brown sugar
- 3 medium-large potatoes (unpeeled)
- 1 egg (can be omitted)
- 8 3/4 ounces plum (ripe)
- 1 1/2 cups breadcrumbs
- 1 tablespoon butter (or 2 tablespoons oil)
- 1/2 teaspoon cinnamon
- 1/4 teaspoon vanilla
- 1/2 cup sugar
- 1 tablespoon powdered sugar (optional)
- dough
- stuffing
- salt to taste

Method:

1. First cook about 500 g | 17 oz unpeeled whole potatoes in salted water.
2. Wash the plums, half them and remove the stones. Place the plums into a bowl, mix them well with sugar, vanilla and cinnamon. Set aside.
3. Check if the potatoes are cooked with a fork, when they are tender inside, remove them from the stove, drain and let them cool. Peel the cooled potatoes, then smash with a potato masher.
4. Transfer the potatoes into a large bowl, add the butter, salt and egg, mix it well.

5. Sift in the flour, knead the mixture until it turns into a dough. If your dough is too sticky and soft, add more flour. Your dough should be smooth but not too sticky and easily rollable.
6. Let the dough rest for 10 minutes.
7. Meanwhile prepare a large pot, fill with water, add 1 teaspoon of salt and bring it to boil.
8. In another pot heat 1 tablespoon butter or oil, when it's melted add 1½ cups of breadcrumbs and ½ cup sugar. Toast the breadcrumbs for 1-2 minutes, stir continuously, until the mixture becomes brown. Set it aside.
9. Roll out the dough with a rolling pin in a floured surface to about 1cm | 0.4" thickness.
10. Cut the dough into squares, large enough to wrap around a half of a plum.
11. Wrap the sugary cinnamon-y half plums with dough, making smooth and tight balls with your hand.
12. Transfer the dumplings into the pot of boiling water, cook them for 7-9 minutes, until they rise and starts to float on top of the water.
13. Remove the dumplings from the water using a slotted spoon, drain them well, then transfer them into the breadcrumb mixture.
14. Coat the dumplings well with the breadcrumbs. Dust the dumplings with powdered sugar if you desire. Serve them warm.

Hungarian Chocolate Mousse Cake Bars

Serves: 15

Ingredients:

For cake layers:

- 6 medium-large eggs (separated)
- 3 ounces dark chocolate (chopped)
- 1 stick unsalted butter (room temperature)
- 1/2 cup apricot jam (melted and strained)
- 3/4 cup sugar
- 1/3 cup cake flour (not self-rising)
- 1/3 cup unsweetened cocoa powder
- 1/4 teaspoon salt
- 1/4 teaspoon cream of tartar

For chocolate glaze:

- 4 ounces dark chocolate (unsweetened and finely chopped)
- 1/3 cup heavy cream

For chocolate mousse filling:

- 12 ounces dark chocolate (unsweetened and finely chopped)
- 3 cups heavy cream

For whipped-cream filling:

- 2 tablespoons confectioners sugar
- 2 tablespoons cold water
- 1 teaspoon unflavored gelatin
- 1 cup cold heavy cream
- 1 teaspoon vanilla

Method:

Make cake layers:

1. Preheat oven to 350°F and butter 2 (15- by 10- by 1-inch) baking pans. Line bottom and sides of each pan with a large sheet of wax paper and butter paper. Dust pans with flour, knocking out excess.
2. Melt chocolate in a double boiler or a small metal bowl set over a small saucepan of barely simmering water, stirring occasionally. Remove from heat. Beat together butter and 1/2 cup sugar in a large bowl with an electric mixer until light and fluffy and beat in yolks, 1 at a time, beating well after each addition. Beat in chocolate. Sift in flour, cocoa, and salt and beat on low speed until combined well.
3. Beat egg whites with cream of tartar in another bowl with clean beaters until they hold soft peaks, then add remaining 1/4 cup sugar, beating until whites just hold stiff peaks. Stir one fourth of whites into batter to lighten and fold in remaining whites gently but thoroughly.
4. Divide batter between pans (about 2 1/4 cups per pan) and carefully spread evenly. (Layers will be thin.) Bake in upper and lower thirds of oven, switching position of pans halfway through baking, until cake is set and firm to touch, 14 to 18 minutes total. Cool layers in pans on racks 10 minutes before inverting racks over pans and flipping layers onto them. Remove wax paper carefully and discard. Spread jam evenly over 1 warm layer and cool layers completely. Transfer jam-coated layer to a baking sheet or tray lined with a sheet of parchment or wax paper.

Make chocolate glaze:

1. Bring cream just to a boil and slowly pour over chocolate in a bowl. Stir until smooth and pour over plain cake layer, spreading to coat top evenly. Let stand in a cool place until set, about 1 hour.

Make chocolate mousse filling:

1. Bring cream just to a boil and slowly pour over chocolate in a large metal bowl. Stir until smooth and set bowl in an ice bath. Stir occasionally until cold. Remove from ice bath and beat with an electric mixer until mousse just holds soft peaks. (If mousse becomes grainy, melt over a saucepan of barely simmering water and repeat chilling and whipping.) Quickly spread evenly over jam layer (mousse will stiffen as it stands) and chill while making whipped-cream filling.

Make whipped-cream filling:

1. Sprinkle gelatin over water in a small metal bowl and let soften 1 minute. Put bowl over a small saucepan of boiling water and heat, stirring occasionally, until gelatin is dissolved. Remove pan from heat but keep bowl on pan.
2. Beat cream, confectioners sugar, and vanilla with an electric mixer until it holds a soft shape and beat in warm gelatin mixture. Continue beating until cream just holds stiff peaks, then spread evenly over top of mousse-coated layer.

Assemble cake:

1. Cut glazed layer lengthwise into thirds and crosswise into tenths and reassemble bars on top of cream filling. Chill cake, uncovered, until glaze is firm, about 1 hour, then cover with plastic wrap and chill until ready to serve. Just

before serving, cut cake with a large knife, wiping it off with a hot damp cloth between cuts.

Note:

- Cake can be kept, covered and chilled, up to 3 days.

Hungarian Cream Puffs Recipe - Moors Heads or Indianer

Serves: 15

Ingredients:

- 6 ounces dark chocolate (melted and slightly chilled)
- 4 ounces unsalted butter (cut into small pieces)
- 4 medium-large eggs
- 1 cup water
- 1 cup all-purpose flour
- 1 cup heavy whipped cream (sweetened)
- 1/8 teaspoon salt to taste

Method:

1. Heat oven to 375 degrees. Line a baking sheet with parchment paper or lightly coat 12 muffin tins with cooking spray. In a medium saucepan, bring water, butter and salt to a boil. When butter has completely melted, remove from heat and, using a wooden spoon, add flour all at once. Return to stove and stir over low heat for 2 or 3 minutes or until dough cleans sides of pan and forms a ball.
2. Remove from heat and stir in eggs one at a time, beating well after each addition. Batter should be smooth and glossy and cling to the spoon.
3. For mini puffs, using a cookie scoop, portion out mounds of dough on baking sheet. For large Indianers, fill muffin tins 2/3 full. Bake minis for 20 minutes, large puffs longer. They should be puffy, and golden brown on top and bottom. The interior will still be moist like a popover.
4. Let puffs cool completely before filling. For mini puffs, fill a pastry bag with a No. 6 plain tube and insert into

side of puff and fill with sweetened whipped cream. Place a puff on a fork and dip in chocolate, or just dip the top.

5. For larger puffs (minis can also be prepared this way), cut the bottom off puff, remove the moist interior, fill with cream, level, replace the bottom and dip entire puff in chocolate or just the top. Serve immediately or refrigerate until ready. Indianers don't hold well -- the puff becomes soggy -- so eat the day they are made.

Gesztenyepure (Hungarian Chestnut Puree)

Serves: 4

Ingredients:

- 31 3/4 ounces sweetened chestnut purée
- 4 tablespoons sugar (add or reduce to taste)
- 1 tablespoon dark rum
- 1 cup heavy whipped cream
- long-stemmed maraschino cherries (garnish)
- cocoa powder (optional)

Method:

1. In a medium bowl, mix together chestnut puree, confectioners' sugar and rum. Place mixture into a ricer and portion out into serving dishes, swirling if possible.
2. Top with sweetened whipped cream, cocoa powder, and cherries, if using. Refrigerate any leftovers.

Rákóczi Túrós (Hungarian Ricotta Cake)

Serves: 4

Ingredients:

This recipe is for a 25x40 cm square pan, use half of the measurements for smaller batch.

for the crust:

- 500 grams oat or any type of cookies of your choice
- 250 grams butter

for the cream:

- 1 kg ricotta cheese, farmers cheese or your choice
- 180 grams powdered sugar
- 6 egg yolks (medium eggs)
- 4 egg whites
- 1 lemon's zest
- vanilla extract
- raisins (to your liking)

for the top:

- 6 egg whites (medium eggs)
- 200 grams powdered sugar
- peach preserve

Method:

1. First, put the raisins in rum so it would soak it up.
2. Now, process the cookies in a food processor until you get a cookie powder.
3. Add the melted butter to it and put it evenly in a square pan. Bake it for 6 minutes and then let it cool.

4. While the crust is cooling, mash the ricotta, just like you would with potatoes.
5. Now, mix the 6 egg yolks with the powdered sugar until it's creamy. Add the cheese to it gradually. Add the vanilla, lemon zest and mix it until the mixture comes together as a cream. Add the raisins (but not the rum). Beat the 4 egg (not 6) whites and fold it to the cheese mix.
6. Add a layer of peach preserve on the crust. After that add the ricotta cheese mixture on top of it and bake it for 20 minutes on 165C.
7. While it is baking, beat the 6 egg whites. When it is almost fully beaten, add the 200 grams sugar and beat it until it is shiny and you can see the peaks of the whites.
8. When the 20 minutes is gone, take out the cake from the oven. Pour the egg whites into a sack, cut off the corner and draw diagonal lines with the whipped egg whites.
9. When you have the lines, drop peach preserve in between the lines.
10. Place the cake back in the oven for 20 more minutes on 120C.

Apricot Kolaches (Hungarian Christmas Cookie)

Serves: 64

Ingredients:

for the pastry:

- 8 oz cream cheese
- 2 ¼ cups all-purpose flour
- 1 cup unsalted butter (room temperature)
- ½ teaspoon salt
- ½ cup granulated sugar for rolling

for the apricot filling:

- 1 lb. dried apricots
- 1 cup sugar

Method:

to make the apricot filling:

1. Place dried apricots in a small saucepan and pour in just enough water to cover the apricots. Boil until the apricots are soft. Do not let all the water evaporate. Add a little bit more to keep the filling from burning if necessary.
2. Add the sugar and continue to cook until thick.
3. Either puree in a food processor or with an immersion blender in a bowl. If the filling is too runny, return it to the sauce pot to continue to cook.
4. Note: You can make the filling ahead of time and freeze it until you are ready to use it. Just thaw at room temperature when you are ready to use.

for the pastry dough:

1. Sift flour and salt together in a medium bowl and set aside.
2. Beat the cream cheese and butter together with a stand mixer or a hand mixer until completely incorporated and creamy (3-5 minutes).
3. Reduce the speed of the mixer and slowly add in the flour. I used 5 additions and completely mixed in the flour each time. The dough will be soft but not sticky.
4. Divide the dough into 4 equal parts and flatten each to 3/4" thick. Wrap in plastic wrap and refrigerate until hard, at least 2 hours.

assembling the kolaches:

1. Pre-heat the oven to 375°. Move the oven rack one setting higher than the center.
2. Take one of the disks of dough from the refrigerator and lightly flour both sides. Spread granulated sugar on your pastry board or work surface. Place the dough on top and roll out pastry to 1/16" to 1/8" thick. Most recipes say 1/8" but my Husband remembered them being thinner.
3. With a pastry wheel or sharp knife, trim the dough into a square and then cut the square into 16 smaller squares. My dough never rolled out into a perfect circle so I would just cut as many 1 1/2 "squares as possible, saving the scraps for later.
4. Place a dollop of filling into the center of each square. I used ½ teaspoon to ¾ teaspoon for each.
5. Gently grab two opposite corners and fold one over the other, gently pressing down to try and seal them together. Gently move it to a parchment covered baking sheet. Repeat with all remaining squares, placing the kolaches no closer than 1" apart.
6. Sprinkle the middles of the kolaches with just a touch of granulated sugar.

7. Bake 12-14 minutes or until the bottom edges are a golden and you can smell them. Let cool slightly on the pan on a wire rack and then move them gently to a wire rack to cool completely.
8. Repeat with all remaining dough. Refrigerate and re-roll your scraps.

Notes:

- You will have lots of filling left over. If you don't want to freeze the remainder, you can probably halve the recipe above. You can also use prepared pastry, not pie, filling, but there are so many additives that the minimal extra effort is totally worth making homemade.
- For a more traditional cookie, you can omit the granulated sugar and dust the final, cooled cookie with powdered sugar.

Hungarian Shortbread

Serves: 9

Ingredients:

- 1-pound softened unsalted butter
- 4 cups all-purpose flour
- 4 medium-large egg yolks
- 2 teaspoons baking powder
- 2 cups granulated sugar
- 2 cups jam (or your choice)
- 1/2 teaspoon almond extract
- 1/4 teaspoon kosher salt
- confectioners sugar (for dusting)

Method:

1. In a medium bowl, whisk together the flour, baking powder, salt, set aside.
2. Add the butter to the bowl of a stand mixer fitted with the paddle blade (or, better, a scraper blade) and beat on medium speed until pale and fluffy (5 to 8 minutes). Add the sugar and mix until dissolved. Add the egg yolks and almond extract, and continue beating until completely incorporated.
3. Reduce speed to low and slowly add the dry ingredients. Mix only until incorporated (do not over mix).
4. Turn the dough out on you cutting board, gather up into a mass, and then cut the dough in half. Form each half into a ball*, and wrap each in plastic wrap. Freeze the dough for at least 30 minutes, until firm.
5. Preheat oven to 350°F with rack in the center position.
6. Remove one ball of dough from the freezer and grate the dough using a box grater into a 9" x 12" baking pan (use the large hole side).

7. Gently pat the dough shreds to even it out in the pan, pushing the shreds into the corners. Spread the jam or preserves over the top. If the jam is hard to spread, heat briefly in the microwave and stir well. You might not need all two cups: use your judgment.
8. Grate the second ball of dough over the jam, and pat to even out the surface.
9. Bake for 40 minutes, until the shortbread is golden. Remove from oven, and immediately dust with confectioner's sugar through a sifter or small sieve. Allow the shortbread to cool in the pan, set on a rack. Cut into squares or triangles, and serve. Store, covered, at room temperature.

Note:

- The original directions call for forming a ball, but I find it easier to grate - and grip while grating - if the dough is formed into a thick log instead. Also, a food processor with a grating disk does a great job here. Form the dough into 4 logs that are skinnier than the chute for your food processor. Wrap each with cling wrap and place in the freezer for no more than an hour. You don't want the logs to freeze solid; they might damage your food processor.

Máglyarakás (Hungarian Bread Pudding)

Serves: 12

Ingredients:

- 5 medium-large eggs (separate the yolks and whites)
- 4 cups milk
- 4 tablespoons apricot jam
- 4 tablespoons strawberry jam
- 3 ripe apples
- 1 loaf stale bread (brioche or french bread)
- 1 instant vanilla pudding
- 1 teaspoon cinnamon
- 1/2 cup sugar
- 1/2 cup sugar
- meringue
- bread pudding and warm vanilla sauce

Method:

1. Slice, dice or tear the bread into small pieces.
2. Beat the egg white with the sugar for the Meringue.
3. Mix the sugar and the egg yolks for the Bread Pudding.
4. Mix the vanilla pudding, the milk, the apricot jam and the yolks.
5. Slice the apples, sprinkle cinnamon on the slices.
6. Add the diced bread to the pudding, pour the mixture to a pan.
7. Layer the apple on the bread mixture.
8. Pile the beaten egg whites on the apples.
9. Lightly stir the strawberry jam in the egg whites.
10. Bake it in middle-low heat for 1 hour.

Hungarian Coconut Balls

Serves: 9

Ingredients:

- 2 tablespoons unsweetened cocoa powder
- 2 tablespoons rum extract
- 1 1/4 cups medium potatoes (mashed)
- 1 1/4 cups confectioners sugar
- 1 1/4 cups flaked coconut
- 1 teaspoon lemon zest
- 1/2 cup raisins
- 1/4 cup lemon juice
- 1/4 cup flaked coconut

Method:

1. Put raisins together with rum extract and lemon juice to soak up the flavor.
2. In a medium bowl, stir together the mashed potatoes, confectioners sugar, and cocoa. Stir in 1 1/4 cup coconut, the raisin mixture and lemon zest.
3. Roll dough into walnut sized balls. Roll the balls in remaining coconut. Refrigerate for two days.

Poppy Seed Hungarian Style Cookies

Serves: 24

Ingredients:

- 1 1/2 cups whole wheat flour
- 1 1/4 cups poppy seeds
- 1 teaspoon baking soda
- 3/4 cup softened butter
- 1/2 cup heavy cream
- 1/2 teaspoon ground cinnamon
- 1/2 lemon juice
- 2/3 cup maple-flavored syrup

Method:

1. Preheat oven to 350 degrees F (175 degrees C). Grease a baking sheet or line it with parchment paper.
2. Combine cream and poppy seeds in a small saucepan. Heat mixture over medium heat until mixture is hot; do not boil. Remove from heat and allow to cool.
3. In a medium bowl, combine flour, baking soda and cinnamon. Stir in butter, lemon juice and syrup. Mix well and add cooled poppy seed mixture.
4. Drop by small spoonfuls onto prepared baking sheet.
5. Bake in the preheated oven until edges are golden brown, about 20 minutes. Allow cookies to cool on baking sheet for 5 minutes before removing to a wire rack to cool completely.

Conclusion

I want to thank you once again for purchasing this book.

Regardless of the intermingling of cuisines in this area of the world, Hungary remains true to its classic dishes. When you visit a gulyás (goulash) on the menu in Croatia, it could be manufactured from octopus. In Austria it's apt to be a stew offered with dumplings. However, in Hungary it'll continually be a paprika-rich soup made out of cubes of potatoes and beef.

Gulyás is perhaps the most iconic Hungarian dish. Like numerous others, it is exotic and simple at the same time. It's so elegant that it's served at elegant Budapest restaurants yet humble enough to be offered at virtually every red-checkered tablecloth eatery in any country.

Hungarian food is diverse and wide-ranging, yet it's relatively unknown beyond your region. Perhaps it's because there are so few Hungarian restaurants across the world and one must get exposed to Hungarian food through home-cooked foods.

By using dishes in this cookbook, you'll be able to produce premium Hungarian food in no time. Now, all that you'll require to do is collect all the required ingredients and start cooking. Select a recipe that hits your imagination and experiment just a little in your kitchen. Next time you have guests over for meals, you can wow them with an exotic Hungarian food that will surely earn them over. Once you know the essential combinations and tastes of elements, you can test out different ingredients and produce new recipes.

Thank you and all the best.

Other Books by Grizzly Publishing

"Jamaican Cookbook: Traditional Jamaican Recipes Made Easy"

https://www.amazon.com/dp/B07B68KL8D

"Brazilian Instant Pot Cookbook: Delicious Pressure Cooked Meals Made Fast and Easy"

https://www.amazon.com/dp/B078XBYP89

"Norwegian Cookbook: Traditional Scandinavian Recipes Made Easy"

https://www.amazon.com/dp/B079M2W223

"Casserole Cookbook: Delicious Casserole Recipes From Around The World"

https://www.amazon.com/dp/B07B6GV61Q

Printed in Great Britain
by Amazon